BLP

THE FLORIDA
LIGHTHOUSE TRAIL

D0829452

THE FLORIDA

LIGHTHOUSE TRAIL

Florida Lighthouse
Association

Thomas W. Taylor, Editor
Illustrated by Paul Bradley

 PINEAPPLE PRESS, INC.
Sarasota, Florida

Inquiries should be addressed to:

Pineapple Press, Inc.
P.O. Box 3899
Sarasota, Florida 34230

www.pineapplepress.com.

Library of Congress Cataloging-in-Publication Data

The Florida lighthouse trail / Florida Lighthouse Association.—1st ed.
        p.   cm.
    Includes bibliographical references and index.
    ISBN 1-56164-203-7 (pbk. : alk. paper)
1. Lighthouses—Florida. I. Florida Lighthouse Association.

VK1024.F6 F58 2000
387.1'55'09759—dc21
                                                    00-032663

First Edition
10 9 8 7 6 5 4 3 2 1

Design by Carol Tornatore Creative Design
Typeset by Sandy Wright
Printed and bound in the United States of America

ACKNOWLEDGMENTS

The Florida Lighthouse Association is grateful to all of the authors who have contributed to this work, as well as artist Paul Bradley, whose superb talents greatly enhance the book. Thanks are also due to Hib Casselberry, Stuart McIver, Dr. Kevin McCarthy, James Dunlap, Neil Hurley, Richard Atwood, Linda Koestal, and Carol Moore for their proofreading and other assistance. Our great appreciation also goes to June Cussen and her staff at Pineapple Press for seeing the merit in this project and for so professionally editing, publishing, and marketing this book, and to Sandy Wright for her typesetting expertise.

We also would like to acknowledge our debt to a number of other people who first conceived of the idea of this trail book and produced an early prototype of it. Without their groundbreaking work, this final edition could not have been created. These include Ann Caneer of the Ponce de Leon Inlet Lighthouse; Cullen Chambers, then of the St. Augustine Lighthouse; Joe Pais, then of the Key West Lighthouse; Bill Trotter, then of the St. Johns River Lighthouse; Louise Yarbrough, then of the Cape Florida Lighthouse; Susan Clark, then of the Jupiter Inlet Lighthouse; Linda King, then of the St. Simons Island Lighthouse; Becky Hughes, then of the Tybee Island Lighthouse; our artist, Paul Bradley; Nancy Hodjis; Dorothy Wiley Jones; John Breen; the United States Coast Guard, 7th District; and the historic preservation graduate students from the Savannah College of Art and Design under the direction of Maggie O'Connor. Thank you all!

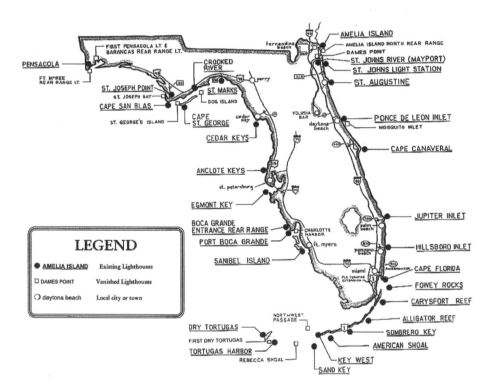

PENSACOLA

FIRST PENSACOLA LT. &
BARANCAS REAR RANGE LT.

FT. M°REE
REAR RANGE LT.

ST. JOSEPH POINT
ST. JOSEPH BAY

CAPE SAN BLAS

ST. GEORGE'S ISLAND

CAPE
ST. GEORGE

CROOKED
RIVER

ST. MARKS

DOG ISLAND

cedar
key

CEDAR KEYS

perry

Fernandina
beach

AMELIA ISLAND

AMELIA ISLAND NORTH REAR RANGE
DAMES POINT

ST. JOHNS RIVER (MAYPORT)
ST. JOHNS LIGHT STATION

ST. AUGUSTINE

VOLUSIA
BAR

daytona
beach

PONCE DE LEON INLET

MOSQUITO INLET

CAPE CANAVERAL

ANCLOTE KEYS

st. petersburg

EGMONT KEY

BOCA GRANDE
ENTRANCE REAR RANGE

PORT BOCA GRANDE

SANIBEL ISLAND

CHARLOTTE
HARBOR

ft. myers

palm
beach

pompano
beach

miami

JUPITER INLET

HILLSBORO INLET

FLA. TURNPIKE
EXTENSION

RICKENBACKER

CAPE FLORIDA

FOWEY ROCKS

CARYSFORT REEF

DRY TORTUGAS

FIRST DRY TORTUGAS

TORTUGAS HARBOR

REBECCA SHOAL

NORTHWEST
PASSAGE

KEY WEST

SAND KEY

ALLIGATOR REEF

SOMBRERO KEY

AMERICAN SHOAL

LEGEND

● **AMELIA ISLAND**   Existing Lighthouses

□ DAMES POINT   Vanished Lighthouses

○ daytona beach   Local city or town

CONTENTS

SECTION ONE: The Florida East Coast

SECTION TWO: The Florida Keys

SECTION THREE: The Florida Southwest Coast

SECTION FOUR: The Florida Northwest Coast

Note: As of the publication date of this book, the Florida Department of Transportation is revising the exit numbers along the interstate highway system. Here's a list of the lighthouses affected by this change and the old and new numbers.

Chapter	Lighthouse	Interstate/ connecting highway	Old exit number	New exit number
1	Amelia Island	I-95/SR A1A	129	373
7	Volusia Bar	I-95/SR 40	88	268
8	Ponce Inlet	I-95/SR 421	85	256
9	Mosquito Inlet	I-95/SR 44	84	249A
10	Cape Canaveral	I-95/SR 50	79	215
11	Jupiter Inlet	I-95/SR 706	59B	87B
12	Hillsboro Inlet	I-95/SR 810	37	42
13	Cape Florida	I-95/Rick. Causeway	1	1A
26	Sanibel Island	I-75/Daniels Road	21	131
27	Boca Grande	I-75/Kings Hwy.	31	170
30	Egmont Key	I-75/I-275	44	228
		I-275/US 19	4	17

PREFACE

President, United States Lighthouse Society

The lighthouses of Florida reflect almost every style constructed in this country over the years: tall and short; brick, stone, and iron; screwpile and conical masonry towers; some located offshore and some on the coast. The Ponce de Leon Inlet and St. Augustine towers are among the tallest in this country. The skeletal towers of the Florida reefs are unique engineering marvels. Florida, along with Maine and Michigan, is one of our premier lighthouse states.

Although several books have been written about the light stations of Florida, this book is refreshingly different. It is a collection of the histories of Florida's light stations by a number of different authors. Each author is, more or less, an expert on a particular light station. You'll find historical facts, interesting local history, and even directions and maps to locate the various lighthouses that dot the thousand-mile coast of Florida.

The entire work has been superbly edited by lighthouse historian Thomas Taylor, one of our nation's premier experts on the subject. What follows is an interesting and accurate account of the lighthouses of the Sunshine State, as well as a handy reference book and guide to Florida's Lighthouse Trail. Sit back and enjoy, then go out and find Florida's lighthouses for yourself.

INTRODUCTION

By Thomas W. Taylor

President, Florida Lighthouse Association

Samuel Drake Adams once wrote, "There is nothing that moves the imagination like a lighthouse," and there are few places where this is more true than in Florida. With a low-lying coastline longer than one thousand miles, studded with ever-changing sand bars and treacherous coral reefs, Florida has long had a great need for the lighthouses that have played an important role in the history of this most southeastern state.

There is no direct record that the early Spanish established any lighthouses in the province encompassing the present state of Florida, although an old coquina watchtower in St. Augustine was sometimes called a "lighthouse" by later British inhabitants. The British also did not build any lighthouses, although they did establish "daybeacons," such as the one at Mosquito (later Ponce de Leon) Inlet in 1774, the one at Sand Key, and the one at the entrance to Tampa Bay. However, after assuming control of Florida from Spain in 1821, the United States government would build forty-five manned light stations and fifty-four light towers, including four lighthouses on inland waters, particularly along the St. Johns River. Seven lightships would also serve on these coasts during various periods of time. Today, no lightships and only thirty light station towers remain, and, of these, only a handful of our lighthouses have been professionally preserved and opened to the public. Ranking seventh among states with existing lighthouses, Florida is, however, blessed with almost every type, shape, and color lighthouse, a characteristic influenced by the engineering feats required to build various kinds of lighthouses on the low, sandy coasts of Florida.

The first documented light station established by the United States in the Territory of Florida was at St. Augustine, the tower of which was first lighted on April 5, 1824. The lighthouse at Pensacola, the first to be built on Florida's gulf coast, was lighted on December 20, 1824. The Cape Florida Lighthouse, the first in the Florida Keys, was lighted on December 17, 1825. By the time Florida became a state in 1845, thirteen light stations and sixteen light towers had been built with varying degrees of success. Since most of the early towers were designed and built

13

by New England engineers—such as Winslow Lewis, Samuel B. Lincoln, Hersey Stovall, and James B. Gill—these small, brick towers were similar to the masonry towers being built in Maine and Massachusetts at that time, without regard to the differences in soil composition, coastal erosion, and saltwater corrosion between Florida and New England. Thus, the survival rate of these early towers was not great, and of the sixteen towers built between 1824 and 1845, only the 1839 Amelia Island and 1842 St. Mark's lighthouse towers have survived.

Just before the Civil War, lighthouse engineers began designing lighthouses specifically for the various conditions found in this state. In 1860, plans were made to build at Cape Canaveral a cast-iron cylindrical tower that could be unbolted and moved more easily than a masonry tower. This kind of tower proved its worth when the Cape Canaveral lighthouse was moved in 1893–94 due to the threat of coastal erosion. In the Keys, where building lighthouses on coral reefs was necessary, I. P. W. Lewis and George Gordon Meade designed special screwpile iron structures that have stood the test of time. Other iron skeletal lighthouses were built on Florida's gulf coast and at Hillsboro Inlet, where erosion might necessitate moving the structures. Cape San Blas proved again the efficacy of this type of structure, as the tower built there in 1885 was moved in 1918. At Gasparilla Island, Seahorse Key, and St. Joseph Point, where the height of the light was less critical, smaller brick or wooden house-style lighthouses were built. House-style lighthouses, similar to those of Chesapeake Bay, were also built at Dames Point, Volusia Bar, Northwest Passage, Rebecca Shoal, Charlotte Harbor, and other locations. The last manned lighthouse to be built in Florida was the Art Deco–style, concrete St. Johns Light Station tower in 1954.

The earliest lighthouse towers in Florida were illuminated by Winslow Lewis's patented Argand reflector lamps, which were fueled by whale oil. However, after the Lighthouse Board was created in 1852, Florida's lighthouses were modernized by the installation of the more effective Fresnel lens, created by Augustine Jean Fresnel in 1822. The first Fresnel lens in the state was probably installed in the new Sand Key Lighthouse in 1853. Soon after the end of the Civil War, all of Florida's lighthouses were fitted with the new lens. Today, a number of these precious technological wonders are still in service, including the huge first-order lenses at St. Augustine, Jupiter, and Pensacola; the third-order lenses at Amelia Island and Key West; and the fourth-order lens at St. Marks. The later bivalve, or clamshell, lens was introduced into Florida after the turn of the twentieth century and can still be found at the Hillsboro and Cape San Blas Lighthouses. The later "drum" lens is still used at Port Boca Grande (Gasparilla Island). At all other Florida lighthouses, modern optics have taken the place of the original lenses. Several original lenses, however, have been restored and are on display at the St. Augustine Lighthouse Museum, the Ponce de Leon Inlet Lighthouse Museum near Daytona Beach, the Historical Museum of Southern Florida in Miami, the Key West Lighthouse Museum, and the Sanibel Historical Village. A couple are in Coast Guard storage facilities.

Florida's lighthouses are a treasure trove of fascinating history. Two of our lighthouses were attacked and burned by Seminole Indians in the 1830s. One lighthouse was blown up during the Civil War but survived. Eight lighthouses were knocked down by hurricanes, three of them in the Hurricane of 1851 alone. The sea claimed four more by coastal erosion.

The lives of the keepers and their families were very difficult in Florida, which for most of the nineteenth century was still a remote, semitropical area where air conditioning and freedom from mosquitoes was a far-off dream. There were many strange, wild animals here as well; one keeper at the St. Mark's Lighthouse was reputedly eaten by an alligator. Often the only transportation a keeper had to another spot of civilization was a small boat, maybe even without a sail. During the 1920s, keepers had to be on the lookout for bootleggers, and during World War II, they scoured the horizon for enemy submarines or surviving crews from torpedoed freighters. Each lighthouse has a unique and special tale to tell.

Lighthouse preservation is important in Florida, not only for the sake of historic nostalgia or heritage education but also because Florida has more small boats registered than any other state. Many of these small-boat navigators do not have modern electronic navigation equipment; hence lighthouses still serve as important aids to navigation. Lighthouses should also be considered important backup systems when electronic systems fail—lightning strikes can completely wipe out the electronics of a freighter, and a meteor shower could wipe out a few of our navigational satellites.

The Florida Lighthouse Association was formed in 1996 to foster the preservation of Florida's lighthouses and to research and publish their histories. This book is part of this effort to bring Florida's lighthouses and the heritage they represent to the general public. We hope that you will follow the Florida Lighthouse Trail and learn about the differences among and the significance of these unique seaside sentinels. Several appendices and a bibliography have been provided at the end of the book to help provide you with further information. You may also contact the Florida Lighthouse Association at 4931 South Peninsula Drive, Ponce Inlet, FL 32127; telephone and fax: (904) 761-1821; e-mail: fla@ponceinlet.org. Also, see our website at www.floridalighthouses.org.

INTERESTING FACTS

ABOUT FLORIDA'S LIGHTHOUSES

■   According to the National Park Service's 1994 Inventory of Historic Light Stations, Florida ranks seventh in the nation in number of historic lighthouses still standing. The top seven states and number of lighthouses are as follows:

1st	Michigan	104
2nd	New York	68
3rd	Maine	64
4th	Massachusetts	52
5th	Wisconsin	36
6th	California	34
7th	Florida	33

Nineteen states have no lighthouses, including Arizona, Arkansas, Colorado, Idaho, Iowa, Kansas, Kentucky, Missouri, Montana, Nebraska, Nevada, New Mexico, North Dakota, Oklahoma, South Dakota, Tennessee, Utah, West Virginia, and Wyoming.

■   The first navigational aids in Florida, simple wooden watchtowers that also served as daymarkers, were established by the Spanish, perhaps as early as 1569. In 1774, the British established the first documented, government-funded structure, designed purely for navigational purposes, a "beacon" or daymarker at "Musquito Inlet" (today's Ponce de Leon Inlet). Angelo Vackiere was the first "keeper" and was granted $24 per year for "maintaining the beacon at Musquito Inlet and for assisting vessels over the Bar."

■   The first American light station in Florida became operational in St. Augustine on April 5, 1824.

■   The first light station on Florida's west coast was at Pensacola. It became operational in December 1824.

■   The first light station in the Florida Keys was at Cape Florida. It became operational in December 1825.

■   Florida's first lightship was the Aurora Borealis, stationed off Pensacola in 1823–25.

■   Sixteen towers at thirteen light stations had been built in Florida before it became a state in 1845.

■   Florida's first lighthouses were supervised by the Collectors of Customs at St. Augustine, Pensacola, Key West, Apalachicola, and Jacksonville.

■   Except for a new lantern, the 1839 Amelia Island Lighthouse tower is the oldest existing lighthouse tower in Florida.

■   The Cape St. George Lighthouse, built in 1852, is believed to be the oldest, completely unaltered lighthouse tower and lantern in the state. The lantern has a relatively rare and much older design than any other in Florida.

■   Winslow Lewis of Boston, a noted early lighthouse builder, constructed a total of ten lighthouses in Florida, more than any other contractor: one at Pensacola, two at St. Johns, two at St. Marks, one at St. George Island, one at Mosquito Inlet, two at Dog Island, and one at Amelia Island. The only surviving towers of Lewis' construction are Amelia Island and St. Marks.

■   In the 1850s, Lt. George Gordon Meade, later to gain fame as the Union general who defeated Robert E. Lee at the Battle of Gettysburg, designed, built, or worked on seven lighthouses in Florida, including Carysfort Reef, Sand Key, Cedar Keys, Cape Florida, Sombrero Key, Jupiter Inlet, and the first beacon at Rebecca Shoal.

■   Florida's tallest lighthouse tower is the Ponce de Leon Inlet Lighthouse (175 feet), which is also the second tallest brick lighthouse tower in the United States.

■   Florida's shortest lighthouse tower, at only twenty-three feet, is the Cedar Keys Lighthouse on Seahorse Key, but it was built on the second highest coastal elevation in Florida, fifty-two feet above sea level. The Florida lighthouse built highest above sea level is the Amelia Island Lighthouse. It was built on a fifty-five-foot bluff.

■   The Pensacola Lighthouse has the highest light focal plane above sea level (191 feet) of all Florida lighthouses. Built on a 45-foot bluff above the bay, the tower itself is 150 feet tall.

■   The lowest focal plane of any existing lighthouse in Florida (forty-one feet) is the wooden, house-style Port Boca Grande (Gasparilla Island) Lighthouse on Gasparilla Island near Port Charlotte. The vanished lighthouses of Volusia Bar, Charlotte Harbor, and Mangrove Point had focal planes of thirty-eight, thirty-six, and thirty feet, respectively. The twenty-three-foot tower of the Cedar Keys Lighthouse sits on a fifty-two-foot-high hill, giving it a focal plane of seventy-five feet.

■   The Dry Tortugas Lighthouse on Loggerhead Key was the first of the modern, tall, brick lighthouse towers built in Florida. It began operation in 1858. The Pensacola Lighthouse was second in 1859.

■   The last of the tall, brick towers to be built in Florida was the Mosquito (Ponce de Leon) Inlet Lighthouse in 1887.

■   The only fog signal station to be established at a Florida coastal lighthouse was at Egmont Key. Around 1910, the lighthouse at Volusia Bar on Lake George in Volusia County was downgraded from a lighthouse to a fog signal station that used a bell.

■   Cape San Blas holds the record for the most towers built in one location. Four different towers, most of which were destroyed by hurricanes, have been built since 1847 to mark this dangerous area. The last tower, the present steel, skeletal tower, was built in 1885 and was moved in 1918 to its current location.

■   The last manned light station to be constructed in Florida was the St. Johns River Light Station in 1954. It was automated in 1967.

■   The Cape St. George Lighthouse (1852) is Florida's most endangered lighthouse. Its foundation was seriously undermined by Hurricane Opal in 1995, and its tower leans 10° off-center. The tower is now receiving repairs that lighthouse enthusiasts hope will prevent it from falling over for a number of years.

■   The first Fresnel lens installed in a Florida lighthouse was installed in the lantern of the Sand Key Lighthouse and first lighted on July 20, 1853. Thirteen of Florida's lighthouses had received a Fresnel lens by the time the Civil War broke out in 1861.

■   Florida's newest "lighthouse" is the twenty-foot classic, red-and-white-striped tower built on Lake Dora by the city of Mount Dora in 1988 to guide boats into the city's municipal harbor. This is a private aid to navigation, but it is Florida's only active lighthouse on inland waters.

■   Florida's "traveling lighthouse" is the 1902 St. Joseph Point Lighthouse. It was discontinued in 1960 when a modern, steel, skeletal tower was built. Soon afterwards, the old, house-style structure was moved six miles north to Overstreet Highway. It later became a barn in which to store hay for cattle. In 1979, the lighthouse hit the road again, this time to a new location in Simmons Bayou, about twenty-three miles to the south, to be used as a private residence. It is being lovingly restored.

USING THIS BOOK

This book is designed to provide comprehensive directions to the various lighthouses and historic lighthouse sites in Florida. In this format, the "trail" follows around the state clockwise, starting at the northeast corner at Fernandina Beach. This is appropriate since the first lighthouse, the Amelia Island Lighthouse, happens to be Florida's oldest extant tower. Also, many of Florida's out-of-state visitors often enter the state from the north by way of the interstate highway, I-95. The trail can be followed continuously in this manner. Directions to each lighthouse follow from a major area highway so sections of the trail can be followed at different times.

The lighthouses in Section One: The Florida East Coast can be found off I-95 with the exception of the lighthouses that are more easily accessed by State Route A-1-A (Amelia Island, Dames Point, St. Johns River, St. Johns Light Station, and St. Augustine). Only US Route 1 provides access to the lighthouses in Section Two: The Florida Keys. For those lighthouses in Section Three: The Florida Southwest Coast, access is from I-75, then from US Route 19. For the final leg, Section Four: The Florida Northwest Coast, main access is from US Route 98.

We at the Florida Lighthouse Association hope that *The Florida Lighthouse Trail* will be of great assistance to our readers in locating and visiting the sites of Florida's great lighthouse heritage.

Thomas W. Taylor, Editor

AMELIA ISLAND LIGHTHOUSE

FERNANDINA BEACH, FLORIDA

By Harold Belcher

At more than 160 years old, the Amelia Island Lighthouse is the oldest continuously operating lighthouse in Florida. It has been active since 1839 at this site, with the exception of the "dark" Civil War years.

The lighthouse was originally built on the south end of adjacent Cumberland Island, Georgia, where it stood from 1820 until 1838. In 1838, the original builder, Winslow Lewis, was contracted to remove and rebuild it on the highest point on Amelia Island, even though this site was more than three fourths of a mile west of the ocean and two miles south of the St. Marys River. Amos Latham, a seventy-eight-year-old veteran of the Revolutionary War, came with the lighthouse as the keeper. He died four years later and was buried on the site; his remains have since been removed to a family plot in Bosque Bello Cemetery.

The light served as a rear beacon for one of the ranges used to show the route into the mouth of the St. Marys River and thus to Fernandina, to St. Marys, Georgia, and now to the Kings Bay Submarine Base. At various times there were three other ranges: Amelia North Beacon, Willow Pond, and Tiger Island.

The original, Lewis oil lamps were replaced several times, and in 1867 a third-order Fresnel lens was installed. The present third-order Fresnel lens was installed in 1903 and is stamped "Barbier & Bénard, Paris." The light was finally electrified in 1933.

The tower is a dual-walled brick structure. The inner vertical cylinder is nine and a half feet in diameter, and the eight-inch-rise, hand-hewn, New England granite steps are embedded in that wall. They overlap slightly, forming a closed spiral much like an Archimedes' screw. The exterior wall is a tapered, truncated cone. The outside diameter is twenty-two feet at ground level, tapering to ten and a half feet at the top. Six window tunnels pierce both walls.

The Amelia Island Lighthouse is not only the oldest existing lighthouse structure in Florida, but, because of the curvature of the coast, it is the lighthouse located furthest west of any United States lighthouse along the Atlantic seaboard, excluding the western Florida Keys. This lighthouse also has the distinction of having been in active operation in two states: Georgia (1820–1838) and Florida (1838–present).

The Amelia Island Lighthouse was placed on the Coast Guard Seventh District disposal list in late 1998. The Amelia Island Lighthouse and Museum, Inc., a nonprofit, preservation organization, was formed to restore the lighthouse, to rebuild one of the historic keeper's dwellings, and then to open this light station to the public. However, since the light is currently closed to the public, visitors must take pictures from outside the gate surrounding it.

▭ Site Facts ▬

Dates of Construction: 1838–39 (present site)
First Lighted: spring 1839
Tower Height (ground level to top of lantern): 64 feet
Focal Plane: 107 feet
Architect: Winslow Lewis
Builder: Winslow Lewis
Type of Construction: conical brick tower
Foundation Materials: brick
Construction Materials: brick, granite, and iron
Number of Steps: 69
Daymark: white conical tower with black lantern
Active: yes

Original Lighting Apparatus: 14 revolving Lewis patent lamps with 15-inch reflectors

Manufacturer and Date: Winslow Lewis (1838)

Other Apparatus Used: third-order, revolving Fresnel lens

Manufacturer and Date: Henry-LePaute (1868)

Modern Optics: none

Present Optic: third-order revolving Fresnel lens; Barbier & Bénard (installed October 24, 1903)

Characteristic: flashes every 10 seconds; has red sector on the southeast

Auxiliary Historic Structures: oil storage house; 1960s ranch-style keeper's dwelling; two-car garage

National Register Listing: yes (part of the Fernandina Beach Historic District)

Operating Entity: United States Coast Guard

Tower Open to the Public: no

Grounds Open: only when gate is open

Lighthouse Museum: no

Hours: none

Gift Shop: no (USLS Passport Stamp available at Amelia Island Museum of History, 233 South 3rd Street)

Handicapped Access: no

Contact: Amelia Island Lighthouse and Museum, Inc., 109 South 18th Street, Fernandina, FL 32034; (904) 261-3464; hal@net-magic.net

Directions:

From I-95, take State Route A-1-A east into Fernandina Beach. Continue to follow A-1-A onto Atlantic Avenue toward the ocean. Turn left (north) onto 20th Street. Turn right (east) at Highland Street and then turn left (north) onto Lighthouse Circle. The lighthouse is located at 215½ Lighthouse Circle, directly up the hill.

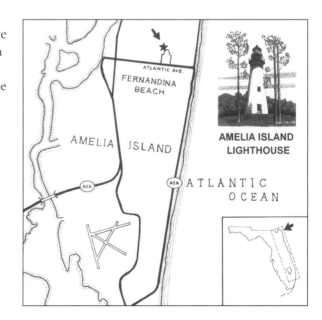

AMELIA ISLAND
NORTH REAR RANGE LIGHTS
(Lighthouse Site Only)
FERNANDINA BEACH, FLORIDA

By Neil Hurley

In addition to the Amelia Island Lighthouse, in 1858 two navigational lights (one a small lighthouse) were needed to mark St. Mary's Entrance, the channel just north of Fernandina Beach. By sailing on a course that brought both lights into alignment, ships' captains could be sure they were on a course that took them through the deepest part of the entrance channel. The front tower was the smaller of the two beacons. Further to the west, the lighthouse, with a small, sixth–order Fresnel lens, displayed its light from a lantern atop a wood–frame house. The lighthouse was located about eight hundred yards east of Fort Clinch in sand dunes along the beach.

With the start of the Civil War, the range lights were shifted to intermediate operation until the lenses were removed for safekeeping in October 1861. Union forces seized the town of Fernandina in March 1862, and while it is not clear what happened to the structures, they did not survive the war.

The "growing navigation interest" called for the reestablishment of the range lights in 1870. Construction was begun in late 1871, and the rear range tower again consisted of a lantern on a frame dwelling. Throughout the operation of this lighthouse, shifting sand dunes required that frequent work be done to prevent the lighthouse from being buried. Changes to the shape and course of the entrance channel required that both range lights be placed on tramways in 1887.

The lighthouse and range were finally discontinued in 1899, when buoys were found to better mark the channel. Surveys of Amelia Island show an "old lighthouse" along the north shore as late as 1924. In 1996, a local resident, Hal Belcher, found parts of a brick chimney base along the surf line in the approximate location of the old lighthouse. The spot was later covered over when the beach was replenished, but, at rare times, the brick foundation of the chimney can still be seen.

▭ Site Facts ▬

Dates of Construction: 1858; 1871–1872
First Lighted: November 1, 1858; June 1, 1872
Tower Height (ground to top of lantern): 60 feet
Focal Plane: unknown
Architect: unknown
Builder: unknown
Type of Construction: frame, house-style lighthouse
Foundation Materials: unknown; probably brick piles
Construction Materials: wood
Number of Steps: unknown
Daymark: white house with red roof and black lantern
Active: no
Deactivated: 1899
Original Lighting Apparatus: sixth-order fixed (red) Fresnel lens
Manufacturer and Date: unknown
Other Apparatus Used: none
Present Optics: none
Characteristic: fixed red light
Auxiliary Historic Structures: none
National Register Listing: none
Operating Entity: Florida Park Service
Tower Open to the Public: historic towers no longer present
Lighthouse Museum: no
Hours: none

Gift shop: no

Handicapped Access: no

Contact: Amelia Island Lighthouse and Museum, Inc., 109 South 18th Street, Fernandina Beach, FL 32034; (904) 261-3469; e-mail: hal@net-magic.net

Directions:

From the Amelia Island Lighthouse, retrace your route to Atlantic Avenue. Turn left (east) and drive a short distance to the entrance of the Fort Clinch State Park on your left. Turn left (north) into the park. There is an admission fee. (At the Willow Pond Trail parking lot, you can park and walk across the road to view the remains of the foundation and oil house for the Willow Pond Range Light.) Continue on the park road until you see the main parking area for Fort Clinch immediately ahead of you. Before you get to the parking lot, turn right (east) onto a small dirt road. Park at the end of this road and walk down the boardwalk to the beach. About 600 yards to your right (southeast) was the location of this lighthouse.

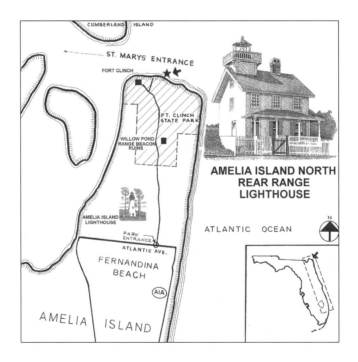

DAMES POINT
LIGHTHOUSE
(Lighthouse Site Only)

NEW BERLIN, FLORIDA

By Neil Hurley

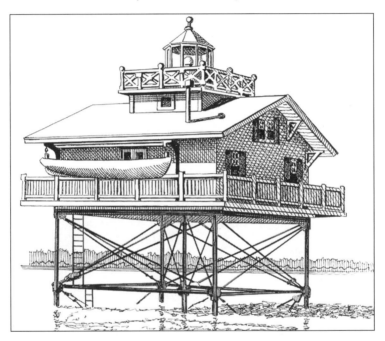

One of two river lighthouses in Florida, the Dames Point Lighthouse formerly marked a sharp bend and a twelve-foot shoal in the St. Johns River between the river's mouth and Jacksonville. A small lightship that first marked the site in 1857, was equipped with both a bell and a horn for use as fog signals, and displayed a fixed white light from a small lens. The lightship was manned by a crew of three: the captain, a cook, and one crewman. During the Civil War, Confederate authorities ordered the lightship towed upriver to Jacksonville. A Confederate fort (at Yellow Bluff), which mounted as many as twelve cannon, guarded the Dames Point shoal. The Yellow Bluff fort was abandoned in 1863, and Jacksonville was later occupied by Union troops. It is not clear if the lightship survived the war.

It wasn't until 1870 that enough shipping returned to the river to merit a light on the shoal. The lightship had cost $9,500, but due to increases in crews' salaries and maintenance, it was more economical to build a pile lighthouse for $20,000. The lighthouse was framed in Maryland, disassembled, shipped south, and reassembled on the site over a three-month period in 1872. It was a wooden structure, mounted on wooden piles in iron sleeves located in eight feet of water on the south side of the channel, opposite Dames Point. During the summer of 1875, Napoleon B. Broward, later governor of Florida, lived in the lighthouse while attending school in New Berlin.

Lightning is prevalent in Florida, and the tower of this lighthouse was struck by lightning several times in 1891. It survived, but the useful life of the Dames Point Lighthouse was soon to come to an end. Dredging and the construction of wooden "training walls," which used the river's current to keep the channel deep, removed the need for the lighthouse in the early 1890s. In 1893, the light was discontinued and the top of the lighthouse removed for use in another location. The lighthouse remained unused until it was destroyed by fire in 1913. Nothing remains of the tower today. As no photographs or drawings of this lighthouse are known to exist, the sketch accompanying this chapter was drawn from one made of a typical screwpile harbor light.

▭ Site Facts ▬

Date of Construction: 1872
First Lighted: lightship, 1857; lighthouse, July 15, 1872
Tower Height (river bottom to top of lantern): unknown
Focal Plane: unknown
Architect: unknown
Builder: unknown
Type of Construction: wood
Foundation Materials: wood piles in cast-iron sleeves
Construction Materials: wood and iron
Number of Steps: unknown
Daymark: unknown
Active: no
Deactivated: February 28, 1893
Original Lighting Apparatus: fifth- or sixth-order fixed Fresnel lens
Manufacturer and Date: unknown
Other Apparatus Used: none
Present Optics: none
Characteristic: fixed white light

Auxiliary Historic Structures: none
National Register Listing: none
Operating Entity: none
Tower Open to the Public: historic tower no longer present
Lighthouse Museum: no
Hours: none
Gift Shop: no
Handicapped Access: no

Directions:

From Amelia Island, follow State Route A-1-A south to its junction at the St. Johns River with State Route 105 (Heckscher Drive). Continue west on Heckscher Drive. Along the road, on the north side of the river, there is a historical marker at the Yellow Bluff Historical Site. Heckscher Drive intersects with State Route 9A, which runs south over the aptly named Napoleon Broward Bridge, a beautiful suspension bridge passing from Dames Point over the St. Johns River. The lighthouse site is in the river just west of the bridge on the south side of the channel. There are no visible remains of this lighthouse.

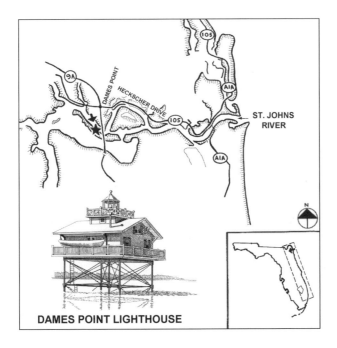

DAMES POINT LIGHTHOUSE

ST. JOHNS RIVER
(MAYPORT)
LIGHTHOUSE

EAST OF JACKSONVILLE, FLORIDA

By Andrew M. Liliskis

The entrance to the St. Johns River has challenged mariners since the early days of exploration. The forces and currents created by the river's meeting the ocean fashioned hazards for ships and shaped the fate of several lighthouse towers. The river and ocean meet at Mayport, the site of the settlement begun by French Huguenot Jean Ribault in 1565. Early Spanish explorers were so taken by the river's forces that they named it the River of Currents. The river eventually received its Anglican name from the nearby Mission San Juan del Puerto.

Florida was still a territory in 1829, when Congress appropriated $10,550 for the construction of a lighthouse to assist vessels entering the treacherous river. The lighthouse was built in 1830 in the vicinity of the present-day south jetty. However, in a matter of a few years, erosion undermined the tower, and the Atlantic Ocean claimed the site. In 1834, Congress decided to rebuild the lighthouse. It was completed in 1835 on a location one mile upstream, where the Navy aircraft carrier turning basin is currently located. In 1852, erosion began to threaten this lighthouse as well, and Congress appropriated an additional $10,000 to stabilize it.

By 1854, problems with erosion, sight lines, and land ownership concerns forced Congress to appropriate $15,000 to build a third lighthouse. In an attempt to avoid the fate of the previous lighthouses and to resolve the ownership issue, the new St. Johns River Lighthouse was built still further upriver. The new tower began operation on January 1, 1859. Shortly after its opening, the Civil War erupted. Union gunboats did not get to use the lighthouse because its keeper, John Daniels, severely damaged the lens. He was sheltered by locals until the war ended. After the war, the lighthouse was repaired and reopened on July 4, 1867. Daniels also returned to operate the lighthouse for a short time. In 1887, work again commenced on the tower, this time to raise it fifteen feet.

The conical brick structure and its technology were typical of lighthouses built during that time. The third-order lens atop the tower was powered by oil and turned by a huge counterweight system, similar to that of a cuckoo clock. At the turn of the century, an incandescent oil vapor lamp was installed, which in turn was replaced by an electric system in 1920. That light was turned off in 1929, and the lighthouse was abandoned. A lightship replaced it to better mark the treacherous river entrance.

Unlike its predecessors, the St. Johns River Lighthouse did not succumb to erosion; instead, the currents of human events have shaped its fate. In 1941, the U. S. Navy built Mayport Naval Station as part of the war effort during World War II. Almost all of Mayport Village was removed. The lighthouse compound and a nearby eighteenth-century cemetery did not fare any better. The keeper's house was demolished, the oil room attached to the lighthouse was removed, and eight feet of fill was placed on top of the entire site. The Navy wanted to raze the remaining lighthouse tower, but local citizens prevailed to preserve it.

Since 1941, concerned citizens have repeatedly thwarted the Navy's efforts to destroy or move the lighthouse from its historic location. In a gesture of goodwill, the Navy made extensive repairs and helped place the structure on the National Register of Historic Places in 1982. In 1997, a community-based preservation group, the Mayport Lighthouse Association, was formed to open the site to the public. In cooperation with the Navy, a lighthouse museum has now been opened, and long-term plans include the complete restoration of the lighthouse and the re-creation of the keeper's house and grounds.

▭ Site Facts ▬

Date of Construction: 1858
First Lighted: January 1, 1859
Tower Height (ground to top of lantern): 80 feet
Focal Plane: 77 feet
Architect: unknown
Builder: unknown
Type of Construction: brick conical tower
Foundation Materials: brick
Construction Materials: brick, granite, and iron
Number of Steps (ground to lantern room): 90 (approximate)
Daymark: red-washed conical brick tower with white lantern
Active: no
Deactivated: 1929
Original Lighting Apparatus: third-order fixed Fresnel lens
Manufacturer and Date: unknown
Other Apparatus Used: none
Manufacturer and Date: none
Modern Optics: none
Present Optic: none
Characteristic: fixed white with a red sector (red from 45° to 187°)
Auxiliary Historic Structures: none
National Register Listing: yes
Operating Entity: United States Navy/Mayport Lighthouse Association
Tower Open to the Public: no
Lighthouse Museum: yes
Hours: Tuesday–Sunday 12–4 P.M.
Gift Shop: no
Handicapped Access: no
Contact: Mayport Lighthouse Association, Inc., P. O. Box 35, Mayport, FL 32267-0035; (904) 251-2410; fax (904) 251-3378; e-mail: beaks@leading.net

Directions:

From Dames Point, follow Heckscher Drive (State Route 105) east to the Mayport Ferry (State Route A-1-A). Take the ferry across the St. Johns River ($2.50 toll per vehicle). Turn right off the ferry into Mayport Village. Go two blocks south and then turn left onto Palmer Street, which dead ends into Broad Street. Turn left and then immediately right into a gravel parking area. The lighthouse is located on the Mayport Naval Station, which has provided a pedestrian gate through its perimeter fence adjacent to the parking area and has given the Mayport Lighthouse Association permission to coordinate and provide access to the lighthouse. The lighthouse is a short walk from the fence.

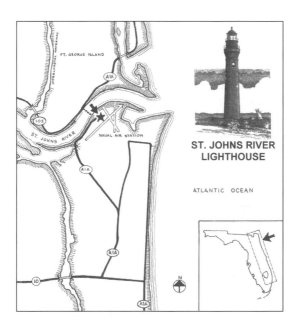

ST. JOHNS
LIGHT STATION

EAST OF JACKSONVILLE, FLORIDA

By Andrew M. Liliskis

The St. Johns Light Station is the fourth lighthouse to mark the treacherous entrance to the St. Johns River since 1830. It is located just over a mile from the old St. Johns River Lighthouse, yet these two structures are as different as the centuries in which they were built.

The older St. Johns River Lighthouse, located on the west side of the Mayport Naval Station, was built in the 1850s. It is a traditional, gently sloping, conical brick tower topped by a picturesque iron lantern, typical of its era. It readily appeals to those who wax nostalgic about lighthouses.

In contrast, the St. Johns Light Station, built in 1954, is an angular, monolithic, Art Deco–style structure originally topped by a small, drum-shaped lantern. Approaching its fiftieth anniversary, the lighthouse is beginning to attain its own significance and charm. It now represents the last manned lighthouse built in Florida and the latest in operating technology.

In the early 1900s, the maritime community began to pursue alternative ways to mark the treacherous entrance to the St. Johns River. They argued that a lightship—with its double set of lamps, a loud foghorn, and a tolling bell—could guide ships into the port more effectively than a land-based lighthouse during fogs and storms. In 1929, after two nearly fatal ship groundings, a lightship was stationed a few miles off the coast at the mouth of the St. Johns as a replacement for the old St. Johns River Lighthouse. The lightship remained in operation for the next twenty-five years, but new technology and increasing costs eventually made the lightship obsolete and too expensive to operate. The Coast Guard decided to return to a land-based operation, declaring that a new lighthouse would be six to ten times less expensive to operate than the lightship, which maintained a crew of fifteen.

The St. Johns Light Station was commissioned on December 15, 1954, to replace the St. Johns River Lightship. The modern, sixty-four-foot, concrete tower was built on a man-made dune on the beach, about three fourths of a mile south of the jetties. It took fourteen months to build at a cost of $250,000. The newly built light station included a white masonry tower; its own water system; an emergency electric generator; electronic equipment including two radio transmitters; a 175-foot, steel radio beacon tower located two thirds of a mile north of the light station; a fog signal off the south jetties; and two modern duplexes to house the staff of three to four people.

Besides the radio beacon with its two-hundred-mile range and the fog signal operating at the south end of the jetty, the light station tower also had an aeromarine beacon of 250,000 candlepower visible to ships up to twenty-two nautical miles away. In the small, drumlike lantern room on top of the tower, there was so little room to move about that the optic was designed to be lowered by way of chains and pulleys into the room below for repair and servicing. In September 1998, the Coast Guard removed the lantern room, along with its 1950s-era lighting device, and replaced them with a flat roof and a state-of-the-art Vega VRB-25 optic. The newer optic has much more limited power and range, but maintenance is simpler.

More information about this lighthouse can be found at the museum next to the old St. Johns River Lighthouse, and access can be arranged through the Mayport Lighthouse Association.

▭ Site Facts ▬

Date of Construction: 1954
First Lighted: 1954
Tower Height (ground to top of lantern): 64 feet
Focal Plane: 80 feet
Architect: unknown

Builder: unknown

Type of Construction: square masonry tower

Foundation Materials: concrete

Construction Materials: reinforced concrete

Number of Steps (ground to lantern room): 71

Daymark: white square tower on building

Active: yes

Original Lighting Apparatus: FB-61A electric rotating beacon

Manufacturer and Date: Crouse-Hinds (1954)

Other Apparatus Used: none

Manufacturer and Date: none

Modern Optics: none

Present Optic: Vega VRB-25 rotating beacon

Manufacturer and Date: Vega Industries, New Zealand (1998)

Characteristic: four white flashes in twenty seconds

Auxiliary Historic Structures: 1950s keeper's dwelling

National Register Listing: no

Operating Entity: United States Navy/Mayport Lighthouse Association

Tower Open to the Public: no

Lighthouse Museum: yes, next to the old St. Johns River Lighthouse (see previous chapter)

Hours: Tuesday–Sunday 12–4 P.M.

Gift Shop: no

Handicapped Access: no

Contact: Mayport Lighthouse Association, Inc., P. O. Box 35, Mayport, FL 32267-0035; (904) 251-2410; fax (904) 251-3378; e-mail: beaks@leading.net

Directions:

The St. Johns Light Station is located on the east side of the Mayport Naval Station. Visitors can access the station by proving Navy sponsorship, by entering the main gate, or by contacting the Mayport Lighthouse Association, which can escort visitors from the old St. Johns River Lighthouse to the modern St. Johns Light Station. To get there on your own, from the St. Johns River Lighthouse, return to State Route A-1-A and go left (south). Outside of Mayport Village, turn left (east) on Wonder Wood Drive, which merges with Maine Street, which runs north to the main gate of the naval station. After entering the main gate, turn right (east) onto Moale Avenue. At its end, turn north one block onto Baltimore Street. You will see the light station to your right (east) near the ocean.

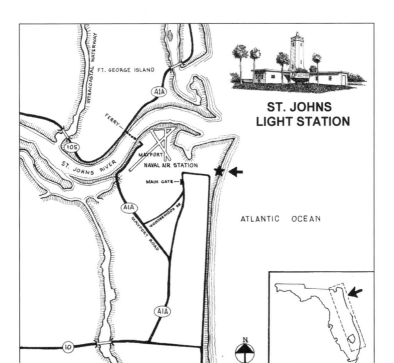

ST. AUGUSTINE
LIGHTHOUSE

ST. AUGUSTINE, FLORIDA

By Thomas W. Taylor

The St. Augustine Light Station was the first established in the state of Florida, and its original tower was the first one lighted in the state, on April 5, 1824. The original lighthouse was built of coquina stone on the foundation of a Spanish watchtower, which itself had been rebuilt in 1737 on the ruins of possibly an older tower. This first lighthouse survived until after the Civil War, when erosion became a serious threat. In 1871, a new 167-foot tower was authorized six hundred yards southwest of the old tower on a site not as likely to be washed away. The architect for the new tower was Paul J. Pelz, who later designed the Library of Congress in Washington. The new lighthouse was completed and lighted on October 15, 1874, and in 1876, a new, two-story keeper's dwelling was completed. In August 1880, the old tower collapsed. Today, its remains are under the waters of Salt Run, northeast of the present lighthouse.

The present lighthouse, that magnificent, black-and-white-spiral-striped tower with its red lantern, proved its sturdiness by withstanding three earthquakes—in 1879, 1886, and 1893—all within the first fourteen years of its existence. The 1886 earthquake was centered in Charleston, South Carolina, and measured 7.2 on the Richter Scale. It was the fourth most violent earthquake in American history and the strongest one recorded in the South in modern times. At the St. Augustine Light Station, keeper Harn reported that there was a loud "noise like a strong wind." Dogs and chickens barked and cackled. "Windows and doors rattled loudly and bird cages swung wildly. . . . Several persons were made sick by the motion of the earth. . . . The tower swayed in a violent manner" during a shock that lasted for about forty seconds, causing the lighthouse clock to stop its movement.

One problem with the lighthouse, which began only three weeks after it was first lighted, was that it attracted ducks and birds. Since it was located on the great Atlantic flyway, the lighthouse was often struck at night by flocks of migrating ducks and geese, which sometimes broke the lantern glass, causing the keepers some cleanup and repair work in the mornings. But it also gave them some sustenance beyond seafood and local crops. One time, the keeper reported picking up twenty-one dead ducks around the base of the tower. Eventually, wire netting was put around the lantern to minimize the damage. Fortunately, this problem does not seem to exist today.

The St. Augustine Lighthouse has always been a stop for tourists. In the nineteenth century, many authors, such as Sidney Lanier, Constance Fenimore Woolson (niece of author James Fenimore Cooper), R. K. Sewall, Margaret DeLand, and Mrs. H. K. Ingram, visited and wrote about the lighthouse. It has also been the subject of countless paintings throughout the years.

The keeper's dwelling was burned by vandals after the station was automated, but the light station was saved, restored, and opened to the public during a fifteen-year-long project undertaken by the Junior Service League of St. Augustine. The magnificent, original first-order Fresnel lens still operates today. It was restored in 1993 after having been shot and damaged by a teenager with a high-powered rifle. Now operated by the St. Augustine Lighthouse and Museum, Inc., the St. Augustine Lighthouse is one of the premier lighthouse museums in the country.

▭ Site Facts ▬

Dates of Construction: 1872–1874
First Lighted: October 15, 1874
Tower Height (ground to top of lantern): 167 feet
Focal Plane: 168 feet
Architect: Paul J. Pelz
Builder: Paulding, Kemble, and Company, Cold Springs, New York; Hezekiah H. Pittee, construction superintendent

Type of Construction: brick conical tower
Foundation Materials: coquina stone and brick
Construction Materials: brick and iron
Number of Steps: 219
Daymark: black-and-white spiral stripes with a red lantern
Active: yes
Original Lighting Apparatus: first-order Fresnel lens
Manufacturer and Date: L. Sautter et Limonier (1874)
Other Apparatus Used: none
Manufacturer and Date: none
Modern Optics: none
Present Optic: original first-order Fresnel lens
Characteristic: fixed white light with a flash every thirty seconds
Auxiliary Historic Structures: two-story keeper's dwelling
National Register Listing: yes
Operating Entity: St. Augustine Lighthouse and Museum, Inc.
Tower Open to the Public: yes
Lighthouse Museum: yes
Hours: 9:30 A.M–5:00 P.M. with extended summer hours
Gift Shop: yes
Handicapped Access: yes
Contact: St. Augustine Lighthouse and Museum, 81 Lighthouse Avenue, St. Augustine, FL 32084; (904) 829-0745; fax (904) 829-3144; e-mail: stauglh@aug.com; website: www.stauglight.com

Directions:

From St. Johns Light Station, continue down State Route A-1-A through St. Augustine and go across the Bridge of Lions. Once on Anastasia Island, turn left onto Lighthouse Avenue directly across from the Alligator Farm. The lighthouse is a few blocks north at 81 Lighthouse Avenue.

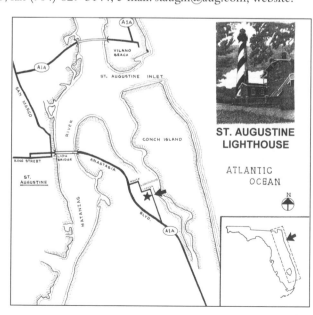

ST. AUGUSTINE
LIGHTHOUSE

VOLUSIA BAR LIGHTHOUSE

(Lighthouse Site Only)

NEAR ASTOR PARK, FLORIDA

By Thomas W. Taylor

When Florida became a territory of the United States in 1821, commerce along the upper St. Johns River was already so great that a petition requesting the construction of a navigational beacon at the south end of Lake George was sent to Congress in 1822. This beacon was needed to help vessels going south on the lake find the entrance to the river in an area where there were no navigational landmarks. There is no evidence that any beacon was constructed, but in March 1883, the Lighthouse Board requested that Congress authorize a lighthouse to be built at the south end of Lake George, where jetties and navigational improvements were being constructed at the entrance to the river at Volusia Bar. The new lighthouse would cost an estimated $5,000 and would benefit some forty thousand people in five counties who were dependent upon ships that navigated Volusia Bar for supplies.

Congress approved the new lighthouse project, but gaining title to the submerged land for the structure took more time than planned, and work on the lighthouse did not begin until the fall of 1885. Iron piles and framework, brought down from Baltimore, were set up in four and a half feet of water, and the white, five-room, frame dwelling, prefabricated in Charleston, was brought down with a working party and set on top of the iron piles. A fourth-order Fresnel lens was installed in the lantern room of this house-style lighthouse, and the entire structure was completed in March 1886. A large bell was installed as a fog signal. It would be struck once every ten seconds in foggy conditions.

The lighthouse soon served an additional purpose. Located right next to a waterway navigated by steamboats, the once-a-week mail parcels for the local residents would be dropped off at the lighthouse, and thus it became the post office for the people living in Silver Glen, on Pat's Island, and in other local settlements. Sometimes, in addition to his lighthouse and mail duties, a keeper had to find additional income to support his family. Captain Frank Lansing, for example, who served at the lighthouse from 1913 to 1933, operated a commercial orange grove on Blue Creek Island.

Soon after 1915, the lighthouse was downgraded to a fog signal station and the lantern was removed. In 1939, the bell was replaced by an electric horn, but in 1943, with trucks traveling modern highways now handling most of the area commerce, the lighthouse was discontinued. The abandoned lighthouse was a popular temporary fishing camp for local residents, and it was also used as a summer residence for a local family in 1948. During this time, the structure was maintained by those who used it, but by 1954, it had started to deteriorate. It was damaged by a hurricane in 1964, and in the early 1970s it was burned by vandals. Today the iron legs of this lighthouse mark its location.

WARNING: Beware of the many alligators in this area. Do not swim out to the lighthouse, even though it is in only four feet of water.

⊂⊐ Site Facts ■■■

Dates of Construction: 1885–1886
First Lighted: March 1886
Tower Height (bottom of lake to top of lantern): 49 feet
Focal Plane: 38 feet
Architect: unknown
Builder: unknown
Type of Construction: frame
Foundation Materials: iron piles
Construction Materials: wood and iron

Number of Steps: unknown
Daymark: white, square dwelling on brown piles with a black lantern
Active: no
Deactivated: 1916; served as fog signal station until 1943
Original Lighting Apparatus: fourth-order fixed Fresnel lens (1886–1899)
Manufacturer and Date: unknown
Other Apparatus Used: fifth-order fixed Fresnel lens (1899–1916)
Manufacturer and Date: unknown
Modern Optics: none
Present Optic: none
Characteristic: fixed white light
Auxiliary Historic Structures: none
Tower Open to the Public: no; only the iron piles remain
National Register Listing: no
Operating Entity: none
Lighthouse Museum: no
Hours: none
Gift Shop: no
Handicapped Access: no

Directions:

From the St. Augustine Lighthouse, return to A-1-A and go left (south). At the next traffic light, turn right (west) onto State Route 312. Continue across US 1, and in 1 mile you will merge west onto State Route 207. Continue on 207; in a couple of miles you will return to I-95. Head south on I-95 and take Exit 88 to State Route 40; go west towards Ocala. Continue on State Route 40 west across the St. Johns River at Volusia. Four and a half miles west of the river, turn right onto a dirt road called Blue Creek Lodge Road. Follow this road for 2.5 miles until you come to an intersection with a sign saying "Volusia Bar Boat Ramp." Turn left and follow this road 1.1 miles to its end at Zinder Point in Lake George. Two hundred yards straight out from the boat ramp, you can see the piles of the lighthouse, just to the left of the wooden guide jetty's end. Sometimes, for a few dollars, local boaters can be persuaded to give you a ride out and around the piles.

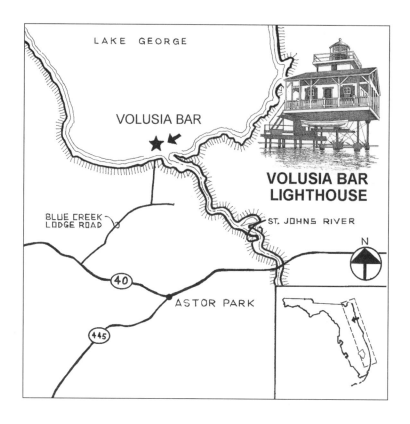

LAKE   GEORGE

VOLUSIA BAR

**VOLUSIA BAR
LIGHTHOUSE**

BLUE CREEK
LODGE ROAD

ST. JOHNS RIVER

N

(40)

ASTOR PARK

(445)

PONCE DE LEON INLET LIGHTHOUSE

PONCE INLET, FLORIDA

By Thomas W. Taylor

Ponce de Leon Inlet (known until 1927 as Mosquito Inlet) is considered to be the seventh most dangerous inlet on the Atlantic Coast. Near this inlet, more than seventy shipwrecks have occurred since several vessels from Jean Ribault's French fleet washed ashore nearby during a hurricane in 1565.

In the 1770s, the British built a day beacon to help guide ships through the inlet, but the first true lighthouse was not built until 1835. That lighthouse was never lighted (see Mosquito Inlet Lighthouse chapter) and was destroyed by coastal erosion after a little more than a year of existence. Indian wars and the Civil War delayed the construction of a new lighthouse at this inlet.

In the 1870s, the Lighthouse Board noticed a large gap in the lighted coast between St. Augustine and Cape Canaveral and decided that Mosquito Inlet would be the best place to build a new lighthouse. On August 7, 1882, Congress first

47

authorized the construction of this lighthouse with an appropriation of $30,000. The noted architect, author, and painter Francis Hopkinson Smith designed the tower. Smith's construction firm would later build the base for the Statue of Liberty.

In June 1884, chief engineer Orville E. Babcock attempted to row ashore from the schooner *Pharos* to begin construction on the new Mosquito Inlet Lighthouse. Babcock's small boat overturned in the rough waters of the inlet, and he and three others drowned. Despite this tragedy, work stoppages due to a lack of funding, and mosquitoes, the lighthouse was completed and first lighted on November 1, 1887.

In January 1897, author Stephen Crane was shipwrecked about ten miles off the coast. Stranded at sea in a ten-foot boat, he and three other men used the lighthouse as their guide to the shore. Crane immortalized the lighthouse in his short story "The Open Boat," one of the finest sea stories in the English language. During Prohibition, Bahamian rumrunners also used the light to navigate their cargoes into Daytona Beach, where federal agents waited in hopes of capturing the smugglers.

In 1933, the original first-order fixed lens of the tower was replaced by a third-order revolving lens, and the light was electrified. At the beginning of World War II, the keepers' families were removed from the light station, and it became a Coast Guard base from which to keep watch for enemy submarines. Several offshore sea battles took place, and many entries in the principal keeper's journal make note of military flotsam washing up on the beach.

The light station was automated in 1952 and abandoned in 1970. Today owned by the town of Ponce Inlet, this light station is preserved as one of the most complete light stations in the nation, with all of its original buildings intact. The light station was placed on the National Register of Historic Places in 1972; in 1998, it was declared by the Secretary of the Interior to be a National Historic Landmark, the first lighthouse in Florida to receive this prestigious designation and one of only a handful in the nation. The restoration of this light station and the development of its maritime museum and its nationally known Lens Exhibit Building make this one of the finest lighthouse sites in the nation.

▭ Site Facts ▬

Dates of Construction: 1884–1887

First Lighted: November 1, 1887

Tower Height (ground to top of lantern): 175 feet

Focal Plane: 159 feet

Architect: Francis Hopkinson Smith

Builders: Orville E. Babcock, Jared A. Smith, James F. Gregory, J. C. Mallory, George D. Benjamin, Herbert Bamber

Type of Construction: brick conical tower

Foundation Materials: brick

Construction Materials: brick, granite, and iron

Number of Steps (ground to lantern room): 213

Daymark: red-washed brick with a black lantern

Active: yes   **Deactivated:** March 1970–December 15, 1982

Original Lighting Apparatus: first-order fixed Fresnel lens (1887–1933)

Manufacturer and Date: Barbier et Fenestre (1867)

Other Apparatus Used: third-order revolving Fresnel lens (1933–1970)

Manufacturer and Date: Barbier, Bénard, et Turenne (1904)

Modern Optics: 190mm revolving beacon (1982); FA-251-AC rotating lantern (1991)

Present Optic: Vega VRB-25 rotating beacon (1996)

Characteristic: originally, fixed 1933–1970, group flashing, six flashes every thirty seconds, today flashing white every ten seconds

Auxiliary Historic Structures: three keeper's dwellings; woodshed/privies; oil storage house; pump house

National Register Listing: yes

Operating Entity: Ponce de Leon Inlet Lighthouse Preservation Association, Inc.

Tower Open to the Public: yes **Lighthouse Museum:** yes

Hours: 10 A.M.–4 P.M. (Labor Day to May 1st); 10 A.M.–8 P.M. (May 1st to Labor Day)

Gift Shop: yes   **Handicapped Access:** yes

Contact: Ponce de Leon Inlet Lighthouse Preservation Association, Inc., 4931 South Peninsula Drive, Ponce Inlet, FL 32127; (904) 761-1821; e-mail: lighthouse@poncein-let.org; website: www.ponceinlet.org

Directions:

From the Volusia Bar Lighthouse, retrace your route east on Route 40 and take I-95 south to Exit 85. Follow Dunlawton Avenue east across the Halifax River to Atlantic Avenue next to the ocean. Turn south (right) onto Atlantic Avenue and follow for about 5 miles to Beach Street in Ponce Inlet. Turn west (right). At the stop sign at Peninsula Drive, turn south (left). The entrance to the lighthouse parking lot is 2 blocks down on the left.

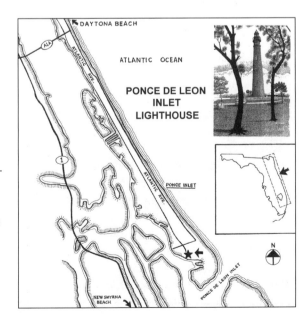

MOSQUITO INLET LIGHTHOUSE

(Lighthouse Site Only)

NEAR NEW SMYRNA, FLORIDA

By Thomas W. Taylor

Since it was first explored by the Spanish in 1569, Mosquito Inlet, known since 1927 as Ponce de Leon Inlet, has been recognized as one of the most dangerous inlets on the east coast of Florida. The British erected a day beacon on the north side of the inlet in 1774, and in 1834, the United States government authorized the construction of a lighthouse on the south side of the inlet for $11,000. This tower would be a forty-five-foot brick structure, surmounted by an iron lantern about ten feet tall. The site selected for the new lighthouse was on a twelve-foot-high, fifty-foot-wide sand dune near a second one on which a house had once stood. The location looked secure, but events would prove otherwise.

The lighthouse was constructed by Winslow Lewis for $7,494, considerably less than the appropriation, and was outfitted with eleven of Lewis' "patent lamps," which had fourteen-inch reflectors. On February 2, 1835, the new lighthouse and its brick keeper's dwelling were completed. Unfortunately, the whale oil fuel that was ordered for the lighthouse lamps was burned when the schooner carrying it caught fire in Savannah. As the oil never arrived, the new lighthouse keeper found it impossible to light the lamps. This would not be the worst calamity to befall this lighthouse, however.

In September 1835, a hurricane struck. It did little damage except for blowing down a few trees and smashing a number of the glass panes in the lighthouse's lantern. To protect the remaining delicate lamps, the keeper removed them to the security of his dwelling until new glass could arrive with which to repair the lantern. Then, in October, came the "high gale," which would spell the eventual end of the lighthouse. In this storm, the keeper's dwelling was completely destroyed, and the base of the dune upon which the lighthouse stood began to erode. The keeper fled with his family to the comfort of his nearby plantation, and the lighthouse was abandoned.

In late 1835, Seminole Indians went on the warpath, beginning the Second Seminole War. The nearby town of New Smyrna was a target, and on Christmas Day, under the war leader Coácoochee, "the Wildcat," Indians attacked local plantations and then burned the town. The next day, they swarmed onto the peninsula and arrived at the abandoned lighthouse. Here they smashed the rest of the glass in the lantern and set fire to the wooden parts of the lighthouse including the stairs. Before leaving, they gathered some booty, which included the shiny reflectors from the lighthouse lamps. Three weeks later, Coácoochee was seen wearing one of these reflectors as a headdress during the Battle of Dunlawton Plantation. After the battle, a local settler found a reflector in the underbrush not far from the battlefield, and it is possible that this might be the same reflector that the famed Indian leader had worn. The reflector remains a prized possession of the settler's descendants and may be the only piece of an original Lewis lamp that still exists in Florida.

Because of these problems with the Indians, engineers could not get to the lighthouse to repair it. In April 1836, its foundation thoroughly undermined, the structure collapsed into the sea. It is believed to have been the first lighthouse ever attacked by Indians in North America. Six months later, the first Cape Florida Lighthouse would suffer the same fate but with casualties.

▭ Site Facts ▬

Dates of Construction: 1834–1835
First Lighted: never (completed February 5, 1835)
Tower Height (ground to top of lantern): 55 feet
Focal Plane: 62 feet
Architect: Winslow Lewis
Builders: Timothy C. Knowlton and Elias Bourne

Type of Construction: brick, conical tower
Foundation Materials: brick
Construction Materials: brick and iron
Number of Steps: unknown
Daymark: white, conical tower
Active: no   **Deactivated:** never lighted
Original Lighting Apparatus: eleven Lewis patent lamps with fourteen-inch reflectors
Manufacturer and Date: Winslow Lewis, 1834
Other Apparatus Used: none
Manufacturer and Date:
Modern Optics: none
Present Optic: none
Characteristic: fixed white light (never exhibited)
Auxiliary Historic Structures: one-story, brick keeper's dwelling (no longer exists)
National Register Listing: no
Operating Entity: Volusia County (site now in Smyrna Dunes County Park)
Tower Open to the Public: no **Lighthouse Museum:** no
Hours: none
Gift Shop: no   **Handicapped Access:** no

Directions:

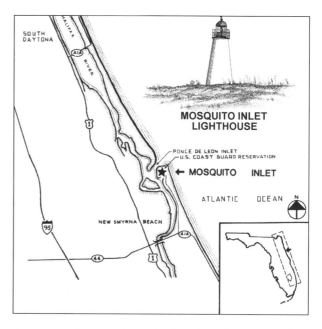

From the Ponce de Leon Inlet Lighthouse, return to I-95. Head south and get off at Exit 84. Follow State Route 44 east into the town of New Smyrna. Cross the high-rise bridge over the Indian River. At the first traffic light on the other side, turn left onto Peninsula Drive and follow this about 2 miles north to its end at the Coast Guard Station and the Smyrna Dunes County Park. The lighthouse was located in this area. Presently, there are no ruins or markers to show its location; however, take a walk around the boardwalk of the County Park, and you will get an idea of what the peninsula looked like when the lighthouse was here.

CAPE CANAVERAL LIGHTHOUSE

CAPE CANAVERAL, FLORIDA

By Neil Hurley

C ape Canaveral was well known by early Spanish explorers and is one of the oldest named places in North America. All European charts of Florida after 1513 showed *Cabo de Canaveral,* or "Cape of the Cane Break" (long grasses or reeds).

Sandy shoals lying off the southeast tip of the cape made the area dangerous for shipping. In 1848, a sixty-five-foot-tall brick tower was built by the federal government. First lit by fifteen lamps with twenty-one-inch reflectors, the lighthouse showed a flashing white light characteristic. Its first keeper, Nathaniel Scobie, abandoned the lighthouse during a Seminole Indian uprising in 1850. When he refused to return to his station, he was replaced by another keeper. The third keeper of Cape Canaveral Lighthouse was Mills Burnham, who served at the lighthouse for thirty-three years.

During the Civil War, Burnham's Confederate sympathies led him to remove the lighthouse's lamps and reflectors and carefully hide them to prevent their capture by Union forces. After the war, he returned the equipment and, in an unusual occurrence, was reinstated to federal service. Even before the Civil War began, a contract was let to build a taller tower that could be seen farther from land. No work could be done until the war was over, so the new tower—145 feet tall and built of cast iron with a brick lining—wasn't completed and first lighted until 1868. The tower was constructed with living quarters inside, but the Florida climate forced the keeper and his two assistants to live in traditional dwellings.

Shoreline erosion threatened the tower in the late 1890s, so it was disassembled piece by piece and moved over a mule-drawn tramway to a site one mile inland. The light was relighted at the new location in 1894. The area around the lighthouse was incorporated into the Cape Canaveral Air Force Station after World War II. Early rocket and missile tests were conducted near the lighthouse. Today the structure is surrounded by rocket launch pads and is in the process of being turned over to the Air Force or NASA. It may be opened for tours in the future.

▭ Site Facts ▬

Dates of Construction: 1848, 1868
First Lighted: 1848; May 10, 1868; July 25, 1894
Tower Height (ground to top of lantern): 145 feet
Focal Plane: 155 feet
Architect: unknown
Builders: West Point Foundry, NY (1868 structure)
Type of Construction: conical brick tower (1848); conical cast-iron and brick tower (1868)
Foundation Materials: brick and stone
Construction Materials: brick; iron with brick lining
Number of Steps (ground to lantern room): 179
Daymark: conical iron tower with black-and-white horizontal bands
Active: yes
Original Lighting Apparatus: fifteen lamps with twenty-three-inch reflectors (1848); first-order Fresnel lens (1868) (now on display at Ponce De Leon Inlet Lighthouse Museum)
Manufacturer and Date: Henry-LePaute (1860)
Other Apparatus Used: none
Present Optic: one DCB-224 rotating searchlight
Characteristic: flashing white twice every twenty seconds
Auxiliary Historic Structures: oil storage house
National Register Listing: pending
Operating Entity: United States Air Force, Cape Canaveral Air Force Station

Tower Open to the Public: no
Lighthouse Museum: no
Hours: none
Gift Shop: no
Handicapped Access: no

Directions:

The Cape Canaveral Lighthouse is one of the most restricted lighthouses in the nation due to its location at the Cape Canaveral Air Force Station and within the NASA security zone. As of this writing, visitors are not able to visit or climb this lighthouse. The only way to see it is to go on a NASA tour bus from the Kennedy Space Center or to view it from a distance from Jetty Park in the town of Port Canaveral.

To get to the Kennedy Space Center from the Ponce de Leon Inlet Lighthouse, return to I-95 and head south. Take Exit 79 onto State Route 50 and head east. Almost immediately, you will see signs directing you down State Route 405 (Columbia Boulevard) across the Indian River to the Visitors' Center of the Kennedy Space Center. Here you can buy a ticket for a bus tour to the southern end of the Space Center, near the older launchpads that surround the lighthouse. Be sure to ask which bus goes past the lighthouse (verify that a bus does go past the lighthouse, as routes sometimes change). To get to Jetty Park for a long-range view of the lighthouse, continue down I-95 to Exit 77, then follow State Routes A-1-A and 528 across the Bennett Causeway to Port Canaveral and Jetty Park. At night, this is an excellent location from which to see the flash of the lighthouse.

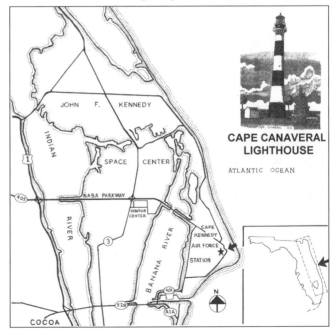

JUPITER INLET LIGHTHOUSE

JUPITER, FLORIDA

By George Blanck

During the Second Seminole War, the influx of military supplies into Fort Jupiter defined the need for an aid to navigation at the inlet. By 1853, a lighthouse site was established.

George Gordon Meade, then a lieutenant at the Bureau of Topographical Engineers and later the general who defeated Robert E. Lee at Gettysburg, was chosen to design the lighthouse. Work began on top of a forty-foot mound but slowed when the inlet filled with silt and five hundred tons of construction materials had to be brought through the Indian River Inlet at Fort Pierce and loaded onto lighters for the thirty-five-mile trip down the Indian River. The Third Seminole War (1855–1858) interrupted the work and led the workers to build the keeper's dwelling with thick coquina walls and an inside well as protection against a siege.

Despite the purgatory of heat, humidity, and insects, the lighthouse was completed and lighted on July 10, 1860. During the Civil War, a group of Confederate sympathizers, including the assistant keepers, sneaked into the tower and removed enough of the lamp and revolving mechanism to make it unserviceable. Throughout the war, the light remained dark. After Lee's surrender, the fleeing Confederate secretary of war, John C. Breckenridge, noticed the darkened lighthouse on his way to Cuba.

After the war, the missing sections of the lens assembly were returned, and the light once again beamed forth on June 28, 1866. Captain James Armour became keeper and would serve for forty-two years. In 1879, the lighthouse survived two earthquakes.

In 1910, discoloration of the structure's brick exterior encouraged the Lighthouse Board to cover it with a coat of red-colored cement. This gave the lighthouse a distinctive, bright-red color, which would be changed back to a more traditional darker red in the restoration in 2000.

During a hurricane in 1927, the electric power went out and the sixteen-year-old son of the keeper turned the lens by hand for hours. The lighthouse swayed an estimated seventeen inches during the storm, and the wind blew out glass in the lantern and one of the lens bull's-eyes. The pieces of the bull's-eye were sent to Charleston, where the lens was repaired and then returned to Jupiter.

During World War II, the lighthouse was dimmed through the use of a low-wattage bulb. Several ships were sunk offshore, and the sad duty of recovering the bodies as they washed ashore fell to the lighthouse keepers of Jupiter Inlet.

In 1959, the two-story keeper's dwelling was torn down and new quarters were built. In 1973, the lighthouse was added to the National Register of Historic Places. In June 1987, the lighthouse was automated and the keepers' families left, although the housing was continued for Coast Guard personnel. Today, the lighthouse is the oldest existing structure in Palm Beach County, and its first-order lens is one of the oldest such lenses operating in Florida. The structure is being preserved by the Florida History Center.

⊏⊐ Site Facts ■■■

Dates of Construction: 1854–1860
First Lighted: July 10, 1860
Tower Height (ground to top of lantern): 105 feet
Focal Plane: 147 feet
Architect: Lt. George Gordon Meade
Builder: Lt. George Gordon Meade
Type of Construction: conical masonry tower
Foundation Materials: brick
Construction Materials: brick, granite, and iron
Number of Steps (ground to lantern room): 112

Daymark: red-washed brick conical tower with black lantern
Active: yes
Original Lighting Apparatus: first-order revolving Fresnel lens
Manufacturer and Date: L. Sautter (1860)
Other Apparatus Used: first-order revolving Fresnel lens
Manufacturer and date: Henry-LePaute (1863)
Modern Optics: none
Present Optic: first-order lens (Henry-LePaute, 1863)
Characteristic: fixed flashing white every ninety seconds (originally); two one-second
flashes every thirty seconds with two eclipses, one lasting 7.7 seconds, the other, 22.1
seconds (currently)
Auxiliary Historic Structures: oil storage house
National Register Listing: yes
Operating Entity: Florida History Center
Tower Open to the Public: yes
Lighthouse Museum: yes
Hours: Sunday–Wednesday 10 A.M.–3:15 P.M.
Gift Shop: yes   **Handicapped Access:** yes
Contact: Jupiter Inlet Lighthouse, 805 N. US Highway One, Jupiter, FL 33477-3213;
(407) 747-8380

Directions:

From I-95, take State
Route 706 into Jupiter.
At the intersection of
US 1, turn left (north).
After crossing the
bridge over the
Loxahatchee River, turn
right (east) at the next
traffic light, then take
an immediate right
(south) onto Captain
Armour's Way. Follow
this around to the
Jupiter Inlet Lighthouse
Visitor Center. Guided
tours of the lighthouse
start here.

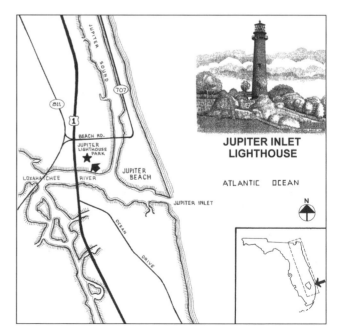

HILLSBORO INLET LIGHTHOUSE

HILLSBORO BEACH AND POMPANO BEACH, FLORIDA

By Hibbard Casselberry

Hillsboro Inlet was a treacherous location in the nineteenth century. There was no lighthouse between Jupiter and Cape Florida. As ships sailing south often hugged the coast to avoid the north flow of the Gulf Stream, they could strike one of three offshore reefs. This is the north end of the coral reefs along the south Florida coast.

Frequent wrecks between 1650 and 1851 persuaded the Geodetic Survey Team to study the area in 1884. Their first request to Congress for this light was in 1886, and funds were released from 1902 to 1905. Beginning in early 1906, construction took a little over a year to complete.

The beauty of this iron, skeletal lighthouse is its lantern room, which houses the beautiful clamshell Fresnel lens. The curved-glass exterior of this room—with diamond-shaped glass panes held with brass fittings—was something quite new and elegant in 1906. Locals still call this lighthouse "Big Diamond."

The Hillsboro light area has had a colorful history. During the great hurricane of 1926, six hundred feet of land between the lighthouse and shore was washed away by the 132-mile-per hour winds, exposing the lighthouse foundation. To protect the foundation from future storms, a 260-foot stone breakwater was built in 1930.

During Prohibition, lighthouse keeper Thomas Knight's brother built a restaurant on an island west of the inlet. Much of the illegal booze aboard rumrunning boats entering the inlet was served at this restaurant, Club Unique. During World War II, Club Unique was rumored to have been a secret meeting place for President Franklin Roosevelt, Prime Minister Winston Churchill, Prime Minister Anthony Eden, and others. They would often spend some R&R near the lighthouse, as would General MacArthur and Admiral Nimitz. To this day, top brass in the Coast Guard still use the keeper's cottages for vacations.

During World War II, battles were fought in the shadow of the lighthouse. German subs patrolled offshore; one grounded on the reefs. In May 1942, the tanker *Lubrofol* was torpedoed off Hillsboro Beach. A naval patrol boat rescued all but two of the crew. In 1943, a German sub was captured close to shore; later another was bombed and sunk south of the light. Stories abound that members of German submarine crews would row ashore in the dark of night and enjoy a beer or two at places in Ft. Lauderdale just a few miles south.

In 1992, the lens stopped rotating because of a broken gear. Some of the 450 pounds of mercury (on which the lens floated and revolved) evaporated, contaminating the air inside the lighthouse. The decision was made to remove all the mercury and discontinue use of the lens. To replace the lens, a 190-millimeter rotating beacon was attached to the east railing as a "temporary light," but this failed in 1998 and was replaced by a Vega VBR-25 optic. In 1996, a Section 106 review was performed by the Coast Guard, recommending that the Fresnel lens be removed from the lighthouse and displayed in a historical museum. Local lighthouse enthusiasts persuaded the Coast Guard to keep the lens in the lighthouse and suggested a new design using ball bearings. With great fanfare, the Hillsboro light shone again in its glory at the relighting ceremony on January 28, 1999. The new bearing lasted less than two months, however, and a commercial-grade bearing was installed in July 2000. Today the Hillsboro Lighthouse Preservation Society is planning to open the tower several times each year for its members.

▭ Site Facts ▬

Dates of Construction: 1905–1907
First Lighted: March 1907
Tower Height (ground to top of lantern): 142 feet
Focal Plane: 132 feet
Designer: Office of the Lighthouse Engineers in Charleston, SC

Builders: Russell Wheel & Foundry of Detroit; J. H. Gardiner of New Orleans, general
contractor

Type of Construction: octagonal, pyramidal, iron skeletal tower with central stair cylinder

Foundation Materials: cast concrete locked with lead and steel bolts to bedrock

Construction Material: structural iron piping

Number of Steps (ground to lantern room): 175

Daymark: bottom half painted white; top half, including lantern, painted black

Original Lighting Apparatus: second-order bivalve Fresnel lens floating in a pool of
mercury (1907–1992); ball bearing system (1999)

Manufacturer and Date: Barbier, Bénard, & Turenne, Paris (1904)

Other Apparatus Used: 190-mm rotating beacon (1992–1997); VRB 25 beacon
(1997–2000) (temporary light)

Present Optic: original second-order bivalve lens

Characteristic: flashing white every twenty seconds

Auxiliary Historic Structures: two keeper's dwellings, crew barracks, shop/garage,
radio building

National Register Listing: yes

Operating Entity: United States Coast Guard

Tower Open to the Public: yes   **Lighthouse Museum:** yes

Hours: call for information

Gift Shop: no   **Handicapped Access:** no

Contact: Hillsboro Inlet Lighthouse Preservation Society, Inc., 2750 E. Atlantic Blvd.,
Pompano Beach, FL 33062; (954) 942-2102

Directions:

From the Jupiter Inlet
Lighthouse, return to I-95 and
head south. Take Exit 37 and follow Hillsboro Boulevard (State
Road 810) east across the
Intracoastal Waterway to State
Highway A1A. Turn right; go
approximately 4 miles and cross
the Hillsboro Inlet bridge. At the
end of the bridge, turn left into
Pompano Beach's City Park. At
this city park, you will have a
good view of the lighthouse. To
see the lighthouse from the
south jetty, take NE 16th Street
to the beach access and walk on the beach 6 blocks north to the jetty.

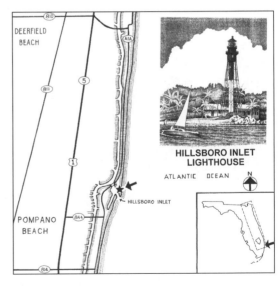

CAPE FLORIDA LIGHTHOUSE

KEY BISCAYNE NEAR MIAMI, FLORIDA

By Joan Gill Blank

The Cape Florida Lighthouse, located at the southern tip of the barrier island of Key Biscayne, is south Florida's oldest structure. It was originally built in 1825.

Shipwrecks and piracy, obstructing international trade and commerce along the sparsely settled territory, prompted Congress to appropriate $8,000 in 1821 and an additional $16,000 in 1824 to build a navigational light at the northernmost tip of the Great Florida Reef. It was lighted by keeper John DuBose on December 17, 1825.

In July 1836, during the Second Seminole War, more than forty Indian warriors attacked and set fire to the brick tower and cottage, injuring a temporary keeper and killing his assistant. In 1838, a military fort and hospital were established beside the burned-out lighthouse. Two years after Florida achieved statehood, the tower was rebuilt on the site and relighted in 1847. As Gulf Stream traffic moved further out to sea, Lt. George G. Meade extended the tower from sixty-five to ninety-five feet, adding a second-order Fresnel lens in 1856.

For nearly the next quarter century, the beacon was tended by keepers and their families, braving tropical hurricanes, rattlesnakes, and mosquitoes on the remote sand island. In 1878, the onshore light was superseded by a screwpile lighthouse five and a half nautical miles at sea. The last of Cape Florida's keepers, John Frow, moved offshore to Fowey Rocks Lighthouse. The decommissioned Cape Florida tower was conscripted during the Spanish-American War as the Cape Florida Signal Station. It was briefly leased to the Biscayne Bay Yacht Club until descendants of the first landowners purchased the light station. Beach erosion in the early twentieth century endangered the base, and a "maximum security" foundation was privately rebuilt for $10,000. When the owners died, Cape Florida was again abandoned.

After a bridge was built to Miami, development threatened Key Biscayne. Happily, Cape Florida was bought and preserved as public park land, with its coastal landmark owned and protected by the state of Florida at Bill Baggs Cape Florida State Park and Recreation Area, which opened in 1967. Listed on the National Register of Historic Places, the tower underwent a million-dollar restoration to its 1856 condition in 1996. The replicated keeper's cottage and cookhouse now serve as an interpretive museum and minitheater.

▭ Site Facts ▬

Dates of Construction: 1825, 1846
First Lighted: December 17, 1825 (first tower); October 24, 1846 (present tower)
Tower Height (ground to top of lantern): 95 feet
Focal Plane: 100 feet
Architect: unknown
Builders: Contractors of Samuel B. Lincoln; Noah Humphries (first tower); Leonard Hammond and Winslow Lewis (lighting apparatus) (present tower)
Type of Construction: brick conical tower
Foundation Materials: brick
Construction Materials: brick, granite, and iron
Number of Steps (ground to lantern room): 112
Daymark: whitewashed conical brick tower with black lantern
Active: yes (since July 27, 1996 as private aid to navigation)
Deactivated: 1878–1977, 1987–1996
Original Lighting Apparatus: seventeen fixed patent lamps with twenty-one-inch reflectors
Manufacturer and Date: Winslow Lewis (1825)
Other Apparatus Used: second-order fixed Fresnel lens
Manufacturer and Date: Henry-LePaute, 1855
Other Apparatus Used: 375-mm drum lens (1977–1987)
Manufacturer and Date: unknown

Modern Optics: none

Present Optic: 300-mm lantern (1996)

Characteristic: flashing white every five seconds

Auxiliary Historic Structures: keeper's dwelling with detached kitchen and privy

National Register Listing: yes

Operating Entity: Florida State Park Service

Tower Open to the Public: yes

Lighthouse Museum: yes

Hours: Thursday through Monday; tours at 10 A.M. and 1 P.M.

Gift Shop: yes

Handicapped Access: yes

Contact: Park Manager, Bill Baggs Cape Florida State Recreation Area, 1200 S. Crandon Boulevard, Key Biscayne, FL 33149; (305) 361-8779; fax (305) 365-0003; e-mail: capefla@gate.net

Directions:

From the Hillsboro Inlet Lighthouse, return to I-95. Drive south through Miami and get off at Exit 1, the Rickenbacker Causeway to Key Biscayne. At the bottom of the exit, go straight to the second intersection and turn left, following the signs for Key Biscayne. There is a $1 toll for the causeway. Continue across the causeway, straight through Key Biscayne along Crandon Boulevard to its end at the Bill Baggs Cape Florida State Recreation Area. There is a $3.75 entry charge per car. Follow the park road straight to the parking areas near the base of the lighthouse. Because Hurricane Andrew flattened the tall trees at this end of the island, the lighthouse is easy to see on the approach.

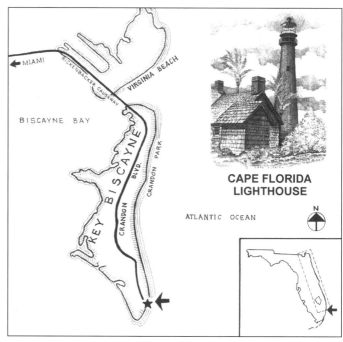

CAPE FLORIDA LIGHTHOUSE

FOWEY ROCKS
LIGHTHOUSE

OFF THE COAST OF MIAMI, FLORIDA

By Love Dean

Fowey Rocks Lighthouse is one of a series of six iron-pile light-houses in the Florida Keys known as the Reef Lights. Built between 1852 and 1880, these navigational aids mark the only living barrier coral reefs in North America. Although these historic lighthouses are now automated and are not open to the public, most can be seen from shore and are easily reached by boat.

In 1875, the Lighthouse Board decided to discontinue the lighthouse on Cape Florida and to mark the dangerous reefs southeast of the cape with an iron screw-pile lighthouse. The site chosen was named, as were so many reefs in the Keys, for a shipwreck. The HMS *Fowey*, a twenty-gun British warship commanded by Capt. Francis William Drake, sank in this area in 1748. This was the fifth and most diffi-cult of the Reef Lights to build. The builders chose Soldier Key, a small island four miles from the submarine construction site, as project headquarters. A work platform was built on the reef site, and launches transferred the workmen back and forth. When bad weather set in, the work crew remained out on the platform. They were provided with tents, provisions, and building materials.

During the first month the men lived and worked under these conditions, there was only one day of good weather. The seas crashed constantly against the pilings under the men's precarious perch. Twice, steamers headed in their direction, threatening to demolish the platform. The *Arakanapka* hit the reefs just yards from the platform and was wrecked. The *Carondelet,* just moments before colliding with the platform, ran aground on Fowey Rocks.

In spite of the difficulties, by May 25, 1878, the lighthouse was nearly completed and workmen positioned the first-order Fresnel lens inside the lantern. Thousands of people had already seen this lantern and lens (now on display at the U.S. Coast Guard's Aid to Navigation School in Yorktown, Virginia). The Lighthouse Board had featured both as part of a special display at one of the greatest exhibitions of the century—the 1876 Philadelphia Centennial Exposition. The display proved so popular that the board decided to prepare another exhibit for the 1892–1893 World's Columbian Exposition held in Chicago. Featured were a painting and a model of the Fowey Rocks Lighthouse.

The 110-foot lighthouse is the first navigational light seen by ships approaching the city of Miami from the south. Neil Hurley, historian for the Florida Lighthouse Association, Inc., suggests that this is why Fowey Rocks Lighthouse was nicknamed "The Eye of Miami." The original first-order Fresnel lens is now on display at the U.S. Coast Guard's Aid to Navigation School in Yorktown, Virginia.

▭▭ Site Facts ▬▬

Dates of construction: 1877–1878

First Lighted: June 15, 1878

Tower Height (sea level to top of lantern): 125 feet

Focal Plane: 110 feet

Architect: unknown

Builders: Paulding and Kemble, Cold Spring, NY (iron foundation); Pusey, Jones & Company, Wilmington, DE (iron tower)

Type of Construction: iron, screwpile, skeletal tower

Foundation Materials: wrought iron

Construction Materials: wrought iron, wood

Number of Steps: unknown

Daymark: brown octagonal, pyramidal skeletal tower enclosing white stair cylinder; octagonal dwelling with green trim and shutters

Active: yes

Original Lighting Apparatus: first-order revolving Fresnel lens

Manufacturer and Date: Henry-LePaute (1876)
Other Apparatus Used: none
Manufacturer and Date: none
Modern Optics: flash-tube array (1982); 300mm optic (1983); 190mm optic (1985)
Present Optic: Vega VRB-25 rotating beacon (1997); RACON
Characteristic: flashing white every ten seconds (with two red sectors)
Auxiliary Historic Structures: none
National Register Listing: no
Operating Entity: United States Coast Guard
Tower Open to the Public: no
Lighthouse Museum: no
Hours: none
Gift Shop: no
Handicapped Access: no

Directions:

Although it can be seen from Cape Florida, the Fowey Rocks Lighthouse is accessible only by boat. If you want to rent or launch a boat, check with the Rickenbacker Marina or with local fishing and/or diving guides.

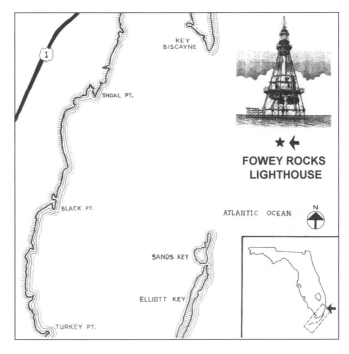

CARYSFORT REEF LIGHTHOUSE

OFF THE UPPER END OF KEY LARGO IN THE FLORIDA KEYS

By Love Dean

CARYSFORT REEF FLA.

C arysfort Reef Lighthouse is the oldest iron screwpile lighthouse still functioning in the United States. Soon, under the auspices of the National Oceanic and Atmospheric Administration (NOAA), it will become the world's first permanent scientific laboratory over a living coral reef. This easternmost section of the Florida reefs was named for the twenty-eight-gun frigate HMS *Carysford*, which ran aground here in 1770. (Years later, the name was misspelled "Carysfort," and it has remained that way ever since.) Charts noted the position of the reef as early as 1775, but it remained unmarked until 1826, when the U.S. Lighthouse Service stationed a light boat on the ocean side of the reef. Violent storms often blew the vessel off station and mariners deemed the lights inadequate. A lighthouse was badly needed to mark this navigational hazard. But it was not until Englishman Alexander Mitchell invented the iron screwpile design that building a lighthouse on the submarine site was feasible. In

1852, a foundry in Philadelphia was contracted to manufacture the prefabricated iron structure. The lighthouse was first assembled at the foundry, then disassembled and shipped, along with trained workmen and all needed supplies, to the reef site.

Originally the light consisted of a catoptric apparatus that included eighteen lamps that reflected the light by means of parabolic mirrors. It was not until 1858 that a revolving first-order Fresnel lens was installed. This Fresnel lens is now on display at the museum of the Historical Association of Southern Florida in Miami. In 1960, the light was automated and is now equipped with a solar-powered Vega VRB-25 rotating beacon.

Even with the most modern technology, the living coral reefs in the Keys have sustained enormous damage from ships. From 1984 to 1989, there were four major groundings near Carysfort Reef Lighthouse, one causing a twenty-thousand-square-foot gouge in the reef, which is still evident. The shock and dismay caused by these preventable accidents were shared by people throughout the country. On November 16, 1990, President George Bush signed a bill that created a thirty-five-hundred-square-mile Florida Keys National Marine Sanctuary stretching from Biscayne National Park to the Dry Tortugas, including both the Atlantic and Gulf of Mexico sides.

Today, Carysfort and the other reef lights not only fulfill their original purpose as navigational aids but also mark the location of the reefs to protect the endangered coral and marine life dependent on its growth.

⊏⊐ Site Facts ▬▬

Date of Construction: 1852

First Lighted: March 10, 1852

Tower Height (sea bottom to top of lantern): 112 feet

Focal Plane: 100 feet

Architect: I. W. P. Lewis

Builders: Lt. George Gordon Meade, chief engineer, I. P. Morris and Company, Philadelphia

Type of Construction: iron screwpile

Foundation Materials: wrought iron

Construction Materials: wrought iron

Number of Steps: unknown

Daymark: dark red octagonal, pyramidal skeletal tower enclosing stair cylinder and conical dwelling; black pile foundation

Active: yes

Automated: 1960

Original Lighting Apparatus: eighteen patent lamps with twenty-one-inch reflectors (1852)

Manufacturer and Date: Winslow Lewis (date unknown)
Other Apparatus Used: revolving first-order Fresnel lens (1858)
Manufacturer and Date: Henry-LePaute (1857)
Modern Optics: 300mm optic; 190mm revolving optic
Present Optic: Vega VRB-25 rotating beacon; RACON
Characteristic: three-group flashing white every sixty seconds with three red sectors
Auxiliary Historic Structures: keeper's dwelling now being used as a marine laboratory
National Register Listing: yes
Operating Entity: United States Coast Guard
Tower Open to the Public: no   **Lighthouse Museum:** no
Hours: none
Gift Shop: no   **Handicapped Access:** no

Directions:

From Cape Florida, cross Rickenbacker Causeway and head south on US 1.
After passing through Florida City, turn left (east) on State Route 997 and the
Old Card Sound Road and go across the toll bridge to Key Largo. The
Carysfort Reef Lighthouse is slightly southeast of where this road would end in
the sea after crossing Key Largo; however, it is impossible at this time to see the
lighthouse from land. The only way to see it is by boat. Many charter fishing
boats and dive boats from Key Largo visit the waters near the lighthouse.
Weather permitting, Captain Slate's Atlantis Dive Center (800-331-DIVE or

305-451-3020) sched-
ules diving and snorkel-
ing trips to the light-
house every Thursday at
1 P.M. Advance reserva-
tions are necessary.
Snorkelers may swim
toward the lighthouse
over the shallow area of
Elkhorn Gardens.
Private boats can be
launched from John
Pennekamp Coral Reef
State Park. Check with
park rangers for current
information on launch-
ing, glass-bottom boat
tours, and sightseeing
excursions.

ALLIGATOR REEF LIGHTHOUSE

OFF ISLAMORADA IN THE FLORIDA KEYS

By Love Dean

ALLIGATOR REEF FLA.

Alligator Reef Lighthouse is situated on a reef named for a schooner that went hard aground here in 1822. Because of the activity of pirates along the Florida Keys, the commander of the USS *Alligator* decided to scuttle his ship rather than leave anything that could be used by the marauders. Both the lighthouse and the wreck of the USS *Alligator* have been nominated to the National Register of Historic Places.

The lighthouse, completed in 1873, marks an area that was the site for a scientific study made by Dr. Walter Starck in the 1960s for *National Geographic Magazine*. Dr. Starck identified a total of 517 species of fish on Alligator Reef, including 19 new species and 60 other species previously unknown in North American waters.

The area is excellent for fish but hazardous for marine navigation. In 1852, a thirty-six-foot-high iron screwpile daymark was erected. Twenty years later, engineers selected as the most suitable site for a lighthouse an area thirty yards from the day beacon and about two hundred yards from the deep water of the Gulf Stream. Because of the exposed position of the site, with the sea breaking heavily on the reefs at times, many delays occurred during the construction of the foundation. Workmen used a pile driver powered by a portable steam engine to drive the twenty-six-foot-long iron foundation piles through disks and into the coral. The hammer on the pile driver weighed two thousand pounds, and the hammer fell on the piles from an average distance of about eighteen feet. Each blow forced the piles anywhere from one half inch to one and one half inches into the coral. The piles had to be driven ten feet deep into the reef. It took workers a year to complete the lighthouse.

Once the lighthouse was in service, the Light House Board wrote, "This is one of the finest and most effective lights on the coast." The board considered the light tower to be the most gracefully designed iron-pile structure in the Keys. Wrought iron had also proven to be a durable building material.

The most devastating storm endured by the keepers of Alligator Reef Lighthouse came on Labor Day in 1935. The wind from the north-northeast was recorded at two hundred miles per hour. The lantern and lens were shattered, the watchroom badly damaged. The keepers saw a twenty-foot storm wave bearing down on the light. The tidal surge of crushing water swept on with destructive force toward Upper Matecumbe Key. Almost everything along the shore was wiped out. In the Islamorada area, 423 people were killed.

In 1960, Hurricane Donna hit the upper Keys. As the storm wave surged toward the lighthouse, the Coast Guardsmen on duty climbed to the lighthouse's highest platform and lashed themselves to the iron structural braces to keep from being blown away. Luckily, no one had to endure the hardship or terror of being aboard Alligator Reef Lighthouse during the 1965 hurricane—the light was automated in June 1963. Today, the light is monitored by a recently developed device that feeds information about the structure into a computer workstation. In Miami, eighty-six miles east-northeast of Alligator Reef Light, someone sitting in an air-conditioned office can read a computer printout and know if all is well at the lighthouse.

▭ Site Facts ▬

Date of Construction: 1873
First Lighted: November 25, 1873
Tower Height (sea bottom to top of lantern): 150 feet
Focal Plane: 136 feet
Architect: unknown
Builders: Paulding Kemble, Cold Spring, New York
Type of Construction: iron screwpile, skeletal tower
Foundation Materials: wrought iron

Construction Materials: wrought iron, wood

Number of Steps: unknown

Daymark: white octagonal, pyramid skeletal tower enclosing stair cylinder and square dwelling; black pile foundation

Active: yes

Original Lighting Apparatus: revolving first-order Fresnel lens

Manufacturer and Date: unknown

Other Apparatus Used: none

Manufacturer and Date: none

Modern Optics: 190mm rotating lantern

Present Optic: Vega VRB-25 rotating beacon; RACON

Characteristic: four-group flashing white every sixty seconds with two red sectors

Auxiliary Historic Structures: keeper's dwelling integrated into structure

National Register Listing: no

Operating Entity: United States Coast Guard

Tower Open to the Public: no   **Lighthouse Museum:** no

Hours: none

Gift Shop: no   **Handicapped Access:** no

Directions:

From Key Largo, continue down US 1 through Islamorada to the south end of Upper Matecumbe Key. The lighthouse is accessible only by boat, although it can be seen in the distance from the Indian Key Fill causeway, where it is possible to pull a car over for a good look. Alligator Reef Lighthouse is only 3.5 miles offshore and affords the best land view of any of the Reef Lights. For a closer look, marinas on both Upper and Lower Matecumbe Keys offer rental boats. A replica of Ernest Hemingway's *Pilar* offers eco-tours of Indian and Lignum Vitae Keys and also of the lighthouse. *Pilar* can be found at Bud 'N' Mary's Fishing Marina at the south end of Upper Matecumbe Key. Call 1-800-742-7945 for details. Many charter fishing boats and dive boats also have destinations near Alligator Reef Lighthouse.

SOMBRERO KEY LIGHTHOUSE

SOUTH OF MARATHON IN THE FLORIDA KEYS

By Love Dean

S ombrero Key, named *Cayo Sombrero* ("Hat Island") by the Spanish, is about seven miles offshore from the town of Marathon in the Middle Keys. The foundation pilings of Sombrero Key Lighthouse, the tallest of the reef lights, sink deep into a shallow plain of elkhorn and staghorn coral. On the Gulf Stream side, there are large parallel coral formations reaching out like fingers. At other places on the reef, there are caves and surprising, twisting channels between coral heads, rising twenty-five feet from the bottom. Brightly colored tropical fish are always plentiful on this diverse reef formation.

Completed in 1858, the 142-foot Sombrero Key Lighthouse was the last of the iron-pile lighthouses built under the direction of Capt. George Gordon Meade, Army Corps of Topographical Engineers. Meade had also been in charge of the construction of the Carysfort Reef and Sand Key Lighthouses. In 1860, Meade left the Florida Keys to direct the surveys of the Northern Lakes. At the outbreak of the Civil War, he requested active duty with the Union Army and in 1861 was promoted to brigadier general. On June 28, 1863, Meade assumed command of the Army of the Potomac, which defeated Robert E. Lee's army at the Battle of Gettysburg.

Before beginning construction of the Sombrero Key Lighthouse, Meade had insisted that the nine, twelve-inch iron foundation pilings be galvanized, a fairly new process at the time. He predicted that these pilings would last two hundred years. Over 140 years later, the lighthouse structure remains in good condition.

The lighthouse and the men serving at it have survived many violent storms and hurricanes. But perhaps the toughest challenge for the men stationed on the Sombrero Key Lighthouse was isolation. Unlike many lighthouses that were family stations, the iron-pile reef lights seldom accommodated keepers' families. Many keepers were lonely and at times found it difficult to adjust to the other men on the station. In such close quarters, personalities sometimes conflicted. One chief boatswain mate observed: "Few people even remotely realize what isolation means to the men living under restricted conditions such as prevailed on these lighthouses."

Civilian keepers served on the lights until 1939, when aids to navigation were incorporated into the U.S. Coast Guard. Keepers were then given the opportunity to join the Coast Guard; many did. The Coast Guard manned Sombrero Key Lighthouse until it was automated in 1960. The original first-order Fresnel lens, removed in 1982, is on display at the Key West Lighthouse Museum.

▭ Site Facts ▬

Date of Construction: 1858
First Lighted: March 17, 1858
Tower Height (seabed to top of lantern): 156 feet
Focal Plane: 142 feet
Architect: unknown
Builders: George Gordon Meade, chief engineer, I. P. Morris and Company, Philadelphia
Type of Construction: screwpile, skeletal tower
Foundation Materials: wrought iron
Construction Materials: wrought iron, wood
Number of Steps: 133
Daymark: brown, octagonal, pyramidal skeletal tower
Active: yes
Automated: 1960
Original Lighting Apparatus: first-order fixed Fresnel lens
Manufacturer and Date: Henry-LePaute (1858)
Other Apparatus Used: none

Manufacturer and Date: none
Modern Optics: flash tube array; 300mm solar-powered lantern; 190mm rotating lantern
Present Optic: Vega VRB-25 rotating beacon
Characteristic: five-group flashing white every sixty seconds with three red sectors
Auxiliary Historic Structures: none
National Register Listing: no
Operating Entity: United States Coast Guard
Tower Open to the Public: no
Lighthouse Museum: no
Hours: none
Gift Shop: no
Handicapped Access: no

Directions:

From Lower Matecumbe Key, continue down US 1 to Marathon. This light-house, like all the reef lights, is accessible only by boat. A good land viewing location is Sombrero Beach State Park. At Mile Marker 50 along US 1 in Marathon, turn south at the traffic signal onto Sombrero Beach Road (State Route 931). After 2 miles, you will arrive at Sombrero Beach State Park, where you can park and walk to the beach for a view of the lighthouse, which is 4.5 miles offshore. The lighthouse can also be seen in the distance from the northern end of the Seven Mile Bridge connecting Key Vaca (Marathon) and Bahia

Honda Key. Captain Hook's Marina and Dive Center (305-743-2444), the Reef Hopper dive boat, and many fishing charter boats, such as the Marathon Lady (305-743-5580), have destinations near the Sombrero Key Lighthouse. Check also with other local marinas for boat launching facil-ities and boat rentals as well as charts.

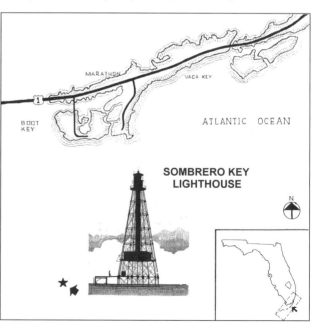

AMERICAN SHOAL LIGHTHOUSE

OFF SUGARLOAF KEY IN THE FLORIDA KEYS

By Love Dean

AMERICAN SHOAL FLA.

American Shoal Lighthouse, completed in 1880, was the final iron screwpile lighthouse built on the Florida reefs. The site originally chosen for the light was Looe Key, named for the HMS *Loo*, a frigate of the Royal Navy that sank on the reef in 1744. The area still contains some remains of the frigate and other wrecks. Looe Key, designated a National Marine Sanctuary in 1981, is a prime example of reef life at its fullest. In an area just over five square nautical miles, Looe Key embodies the diversity of plant and animal life that snorkelers as well as advanced divers come to see. The American Shoal Lighthouse, southwest of Looe Key, is almost identical in design to the Fowey Rocks Lighthouse off Miami, without the Victorian flourishes and bell-shaped dome. This stark and sturdy-looking lighthouse was honored by the United States Postal Service in its American lighthouses postage stamp series issued on April 26, 1990.

The lighthouse served not only as an important navigational aid but also as a Coast Guard radar/visual station during the Cuban refugee exodus of 1980. Six Coast Guardsmen were assigned to the lighthouse during that time, and the lighthouse continued to operate automatically as a lighted beacon. At the completion of the exodus, Lt. R. C. Eccles reported, "There is no doubt in my mind that these lights can be effectively utilized to put another small dent in the tremendous flow of illegal maritime activity that transpires in and around the Keys."

The need for a navigational marker on American Shoal was recognized in 1850, when a thirty-six-foot-high iron screwpile was erected as a daymark. But more than daymarks and lighted aids are needed to prevent vessels from going aground on the coral reefs. Recently the Coast Guard's Aid to Navigation (ATON) personnel installed radar beacons (RACONs) on American Shoal Lighthouse and the other five reef lights. RACONs produce a distinctive image on the screens of radar sets and are visible to most commercial shipboard radar systems six to twenty miles from the lighthouses. These devices are of great benefit to mariners in preventing groundings and provide valuable protection for the living reef and marine environment.

▭ Site Facts ▬

Dates of Construction: 1879–1880
First Lighted: July 15, 1880
Tower Height (from sea bottom to top of lantern): 124 feet
Focal Plane: 109 feet
Architect: unknown
Builders: Phoenix Iron Company, Trenton, NJ
Type of Construction: iron screwpile
Foundation Materials: wrought iron
Number of Steps: unknown
Day Mark: brown octagonal pyramidal skeletal tower enclosing white staircase and
    brown octagonal dwelling; pile foundation
Active: yes
Automated: 1963
Original Lighting Apparatus: first-order revolving Fresnel lens (removed in 1980)
Manufacturer and Date: Henry-LePaute (1874)
Other Apparatus Used: none
Manufacturer and Date: none
Modern Optics: 190mm revolving lantern
Present Optic: Vega VRB-25 revolving beacon; RACON
Characteristic: three-group flashing white every fifteen seconds with two red sectors
Auxiliary Historic Structures: keeper's dwelling integrated into structure
National Register Listing: no

Operating Entity: United States Coast Guard
Tower Open to the Public: no
Lighthouse Museum: no
Hours: none
Gift Shop: no
Handicapped Access: no

Directions:

From the Seven Mile Bridge, continue down US 1 to Sugarloaf Key. The lighthouse is accessible only by boat but can be seen from shore. After crossing Bow Channel onto Sugarloaf Key, continue about 3 miles to the intersection of Sugarloaf Boulevard (State Route 939). The Sugarloaf Lodge will be on your right. Turn left (south) and follow Sugarloaf Boulevard for 5.2 miles to a small concrete bridge near the end of the road. From this bridge is the best land view of American Shoal Lighthouse. Occasionally, charter boat captains take visitors out to the lighthouse. Check with marinas on Little Torch Key, Cudjoe Key, and Sugarloaf Key for boat rentals and charters. Anglers use the American Shoal Lighthouse as a marker for good fishing, and snorkelers and divers find Looe Key and American Shoal excellent sites for viewing tropical reef fish.

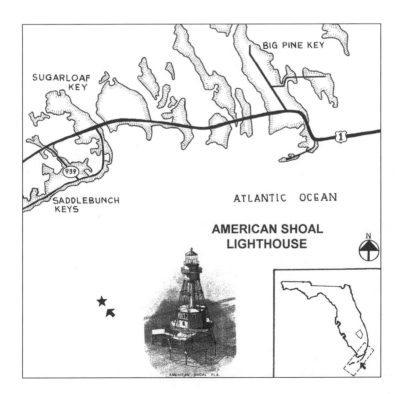

KEY WEST LIGHTHOUSE

KEY WEST, FLORIDA

By Thomas W. Taylor

The first lighthouse at Key West was lighted on March 10, 1826. Described by the local superintendent of lights as "unquestionably one of the best lights in the U. States," this tower was destroyed by a hurricane in 1846. Recently, the foundations of the tower, which were long believed to have been washed out to sea, were found on Whitehead Point. A second lighthouse was built further inland on a more sheltered hill, fifteen feet above sea level, about halfway up today's Whitehead Street. The first lighthouse built within the limits of a city, its thirteen whale oil lamps were first lighted on January 15, 1848. In 1858, a magnificent Henry-LePaute third-order Fresnel lens, which serves in the tower to this day, was installed.

The keeper of the new lighthouse, Barbara Mabrity, had succeeded her husband as keeper of the old lighthouse in 1832. She served at the new lighthouse until 1864, possibly when pro-Confederate statements were attributed to her and, at the age of eighty-two, she was encouraged to retire from her position by federal officials. Staunch Barbara Mabrity, one of the true legends of women lighthouse keepers, has been remembered, and a new Coast Guard buoy tender has been named for her. Her granddaughter married a later keeper, then succeeded him as keeper. Some people believe that later one of Barbara Mabrity's grandsons became keeper and that his wife succeeded him. If this is true, Barbara Mabrity and her grandchildren or their spouses kept the Key West Lighthouse for eighty-two of the eighty-nine years it was a manned station!

During the nineteenth century, there were many changes at the Key West Lighthouse. It received a new lantern in 1873. In 1887, a new keeper's dwelling, which still exists, was constructed. In 1895, the tower was extended twenty feet, and another new lantern was mounted on top. In 1898, the lighthouse witnessed the arrival of the battleship *Maine* on its way to Havana harbor and its destiny.

Hurricanes devastated Key West many times in the past century, but the lighthouse endured them all. In 1915, the lighthouse was automated. The keeper's dwelling, no longer inhabited by keepers, was used as housing for the superintendent of the Seventh Lighthouse District.

Throughout the twentieth century, the lighthouse was a destination for visitors. One who came to visit decided to stay. He purchased a house across the street from the lighthouse, and the fixed white light would shine into his bedroom window. The new Key West resident was Ernest Hemingway. Legend later reported that he sometimes wrote under the huge false Banyan tree next to the lighthouse tower.

The lighthouse was decommissioned in 1969, after 121 years of service. Thanks to the Key West Art and Historical Society, the tower and keeper's dwelling have been restored and are open to the public. The lighthouse is a sight every visitor to Key West must see.

▭ Site Facts ▬

Date of Construction: 1847
First Lighted: January 15, 1848
Tower Height (ground to top of lantern): 86 feet (originally 60 feet)
Focal Plane: 91 feet (originally 67 feet)
Architect: Smith, Keeney, and Hollowday Co.
Builder: Duncan Cameron
Type of Construction: conical masonry tower
Foundation Materials: brick
Construction Materials: brick, granite, and iron
Number of Steps: 98
Daymark: whitewashed conical brick tower with black lantern
Active: No

Deactivated: December 1, 1969

Original Lighting Apparatus: thirteen Lewis patent lamps with twenty-one-inch reflectors (1847–1858)

Manufacturer and Date: Winslow Lewis (1847)

Other Apparatus Used: third-order fixed Fresnel lens (1859–present)

Manufacturer and Date: Henry-LePaute (1858)

Modern Optics: none

Present Optic: original third-order fixed Fresnel lens (1858)

Characteristic: fixed, white light

Auxiliary Historic Structures: keeper's dwelling, privy, oil storage house, chicken coop

National Register Listing: yes

Operating Entity: Key West Art and Historical Society, Inc.

Tower Open to the Public: yes

Lighthouse Museum: yes

Hours: Daily 9:30 A.M.–5:00 P.M.

Gift Shop: yes

Handicapped Access: yes

Contact: Key West Art and Historical Society, Inc., 281 Front Street, Key West, FL 33040; (305) 295-6616

Directions:

After viewing the American Shoal Lighthouse, continue down US 1 into Key West. Follow it (as Truman Street) through the city to its intersection with Whitehead Street. The lighthouse is on the northwest corner. Go through the intersection and enter the parking area on your right.

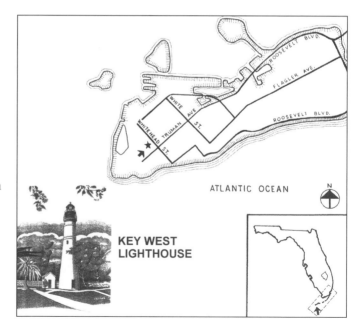

KEY WEST LIGHTHOUSE

SAND KEY LIGHTHOUSE

OFF KEY WEST IN THE FLORIDA KEYS

By Love Dean

U nlike the other reef lights, the Sand Key Lighthouse has never been considered an isolated station. It is located nine miles south-southwest of the harbor of Key West on a small, white, sandy islet that often changes shape and sometimes disappears completely. As Key West developed, shipping activity in the vicinity of the light increased. Turtlers, fishermen, and wreckers often stopped on the island to collect birds' eggs and to socialize. It has always been an enticing spot to picnic.

The first brick light tower on the island, built in 1827, survived the officially recorded hurricanes of 1835, 1841, 1842, and 1844. But in 1846, storm waves surged over the island. The keeper's house and the light tower collapsed, killing the keeper and five others who had fled to the tower for safety. Sand Key disappeared and a lightship, the *Honey*, was moored nearby. It remained on station for seven years. Knowing the instability of the site, lighthouse engineers decided to erect a wrought-iron screwpile lighthouse on Sand Key, with foundation piles secured to the underwater coral reefs. Work began under chief engineer Lt. George Gordon Meade, who would eventually build or work on seven lighthouses in Florida. Meade's work at Sand Key has given him a measure of immortality, as the lighthouse has withstood all subsequent hurricanes even though the island has been washed away many times.

What almost destroyed the Sand Key Lighthouse was a devastating fire in 1989. The damage was concentrated in the central core of the tower, and the Coast Guard concluded that the tower was still serviceable and should be salvaged. Renovations took about ten years, but—sans stairwell and keeper's house—the Sand Key Lighthouse still stands and once again functions as an essential lighted aid to navigation.

◻ Site Facts ◼

Dates of Construction: 1852–1853
First Lighted: July 20, 1853
Tower Height (sea bottom to top of lantern): 132 feet
Focal Plane: 109 feet
Architect: I. W. P. Lewis
Builders: Lt. George Gordon Meade, chief engineer; J. V. Merrick and Son; (lantern and watchroom); John F. Riley Iron Works, Charleston, SC
Type of Construction: iron screwpile
Foundation Materials: wrought iron
Construction Materials: wrought iron, wood
Number of Steps: 112
Daymark: brown, square pyramidal skeletal tower with white lantern
Active: yes
Deactivated: 1989–1996 (during restoration)
Original Lighting Apparatus: revolving first-order Fresnel (removed 1982)
Manufacturer and Date: Henry-LePaute (1853)
Other Apparatus Used: none
Manufacturer and Date: none
Modern Optics: flash tube arrays (1982); flashing 300mm optic (1983); rotating 190mm optic (1987)
Present Optic: Vega VRB-25 rotating beacon
Characteristic: two-group flashing white every fifteen seconds
Auxiliary Historic Structures: none (keeper's dwelling and stair cylinder removed during restoration)
National Register Listing: yes
Operating Entity: United States Coast Guard

Tower Open to the Public: no
Lighthouse Museum: no
Hours: none
Gift Shop: none
Handicapped Access: no

Directions:

Like all Reef Lights, this lighthouse is accessible only by boat. On some very clear days, it can be seen in the distance from the south end of the beach of Fort Zachary Taylor State Park on the southwest tip of Key West. Many dive shops in Key West take snorkelers and divers to Sand Key, and you will definitely see the lighthouse if you take a fishing charter. Sunny Days Catamarans (located at the corner of Greene and Elizabeth Streets in Key West, 1-800-236-7937) has a boat that goes out to Sand Key. Check the local marinas in Key West for suggestions on charter boats and boat rentals.

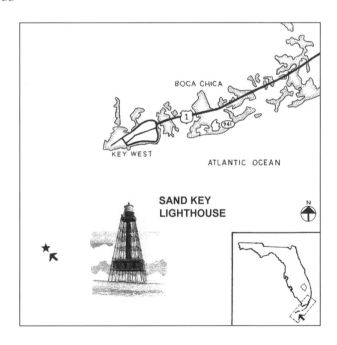

NORTHWEST PASSAGE LIGHTHOUSE

(Lighthouse Ruins Only)

NEAR KEY WEST, FLORIDA

By Neil Hurley

As early as 1833, mariners were petitioning Congress for a lighthouse to mark the Northwest Passage into Key West. The twelve-foot-deep passage could be used as a shortcut for vessels going from the Atlantic to ports in the Gulf of Mexico. The outer entrance to the channel is in open water, with no land or islands nearby.

In 1838, a 145-ton lightship named the *Key West* was anchored to mark the entrance to the channel, located about seven miles from Key West. The lightship was poorly built and the light had a poor reputation during most of its operation. In the hurricane of 1846, the anchor chain broke and the ship was pushed sixty miles to the north before it could sail back to its station.

By 1850, the high cost of maintaining the lightship made a lighthouse preferable, and in 1854, work began on a small wooden lighthouse on iron piles. The dwelling section of the structure was prefabricated in Philadelphia and shipped down to the site for assembly. Yellow fever epidemics and rough sea conditions delayed completion of the lighthouse until 1855. A keeper and two assistants manned the structure. Like other Key West area lighthouses, the Northwest Passage Lighthouse remained in operation throughout the Civil War.

Because of wood rot, the entire wooden part of the lighthouse was replaced in 1879. During an inspection of the lighthouse in 1911, it was recommended that the light be converted to acetylene gas and the station be unmanned. The light continued to operate until around 1921, when the iron lantern was removed and the hole roofed over. The deserted structure remained standing alongside the channel. Local rumor eventually and erroneously labeled it as one of Ernest Hemingway's homes. In 1971, it was destroyed by fire, and today only the iron foundation pilings remain. It's easy to see the pilings, which lie in four feet of water on the west side of the channel entrance, about seven miles northwest of Key West.

Site Facts

Dates of Construction: 1854–1855
First Lighted: March 5, 1855
Tower Height: unknown
Focal Plane: 47 feet
Architect: unknown
Builders: unknown
Type of Construction: wood, house-style lighthouse on iron screwpiles
Foundation Materials: iron screwpiles
Construction Materials: wood and iron
Number of Steps: unknown
Daymark: white house with brown piles and black lantern
Active: no
Deactivated: 1921
Original Lighting Apparatus: fifth-order fixed Fresnel lens
Manufacturer and Date: L. Sautter (1854)
Other Apparatus Used: none
Present Optics: none
Characteristic: fixed white light
Auxiliary Historic Structures: none
National Register Listing: no
Operating Entity: United States Coast Guard
Tower Open to the Public: no

Lighthouse Museum: no
Hours: none
Gift Shop: none
Handicapped Access: no

Directions:

These lighthouse ruins are located about 7 miles northwest of Key West and can be reached only by boat. Check with charter boat companies in Key West. Tour boats to the Dry Tortugas often pass close enough to see these ruins.

REBECCA SHOAL LIGHTHOUSE

WEST OF KEY WEST, FLORIDA

By Thomas W. Taylor

The lighthouse on Rebecca Shoal was the last and most difficult built in the Florida Keys. It was located forty-three miles west of Key West in very turbulent waters. Efforts to construct a day beacon here began in 1854, when Lt. George Gordon Meade came to inspect the site. He commented that no beacon of any kind had been erected, in the United States or in Europe, in a position that was more exposed or offered greater obstacles. The beacon was nearly completed when, on May 17, 1855, a violent storm washed the entire structure away. Several times, work on a beacon here continued, and each time the structure failed to survive storms. The shoal was finally marked with buoys rather than a day beacon.

The Civil War delayed any further work on the beacon, but finally, in May 1873, one was completed. It was destroyed that October. Bad weather made reconstruction impossible until the Lighthouse Board finally decided that a major structure would be needed to mark this dangerous shoal. In 1879, a seventy-five-foot-high skeletal beacon was assembled at Key West, taken apart, then reassembled on Rebecca Shoal. However, more than just a daymark was needed here. In May 1886, the seventy-five-foot tower was taken down, and work began on the lighthouse. The new house-style lighthouse on screwpile pilings was first lighted on November 1, 1886, sending out a light that flashed alternately red and white.

The lighthouse consisted of three floors, with the lantern incorporated into the roof of the structure. Supplies were lifted onto the first floor by a small crane. The three keepers—all men without their families—lived on the second floor. The third floor was a single room with four dormer windows that served as the service and repair room for the lamp and lens and as the watchroom.

This lighthouse survived many severe storms. In 1889, one storm rocked the lighthouse so badly that the lens was damaged. In 1893, the red-and-white flashing lens was changed to a white lens; red sector panels were installed so that a red flash could only be seen when a vessel was approaching a dangerous reef.

Sometimes, tragic things happened at Rebecca Shoal. In 1902, perhaps because of the extreme remoteness of this lighthouse, one of the assistant keepers went out of his mind and either fell or jumped into the water below, never to be seen again. The following year, the principal keeper died there.

On August 1, 1925, the Rebecca Shoal Lighthouse was automated by the acetylene gas system, and keepers no longer had to risk their lives there. But deterioration and vandalism took their toll on the structure, and in 1953, the house was removed. In 1985, the entire structure was replaced, and today, the Rebecca Shoal Lighthouse is an automated beacon mounted directly on a new screwpile foundation.

⊏⊐ Site Facts ▬▬

Date of Construction: 1886
First Lighted: November 1, 1886
Tower Height (sea bottom to top of lantern): 82 feet
Focal Plane: 66 feet
Architect: unknown
Builders: unknown
Type of Construction: house-style lighthouse on iron screwpiles
Foundation Materials: iron screwpiles
Construction Materials: wood and iron
Number of Steps: unknown
Daymark: white dwelling on brown pile foundation with black lantern
Active: yes (replacement structure)
Original Lighting Apparatus: fourth-order revolving Fresnel lens (1886)
Manufacturer and Date: unknown

Other Apparatus Used: fourth-order Fresnel lens (1889)
Manufacturer and Date: unknown
Modern Optics: solar-powered Amerace 190mm rotating beacon
Present Optic: solar-powered 250mm lantern
Characteristic: red-and-white flashing light (originally) flashing white every six seconds
    with one red sector (currently)
Auxiliary Historic Structures: none
National Register Listing: no
Operating Entity: United States Coast Guard
Tower Open to the Public: no
Lighthouse Museum: no
Hours: none
Gift Shop: no
Handicapped Access: no

Directions:

This lighthouse is accessible only by boat. Several boat charters and boat ramps are available in Key West, and the daily tour boats to the Dry Tortugas make runs past the remains of this lighthouse.

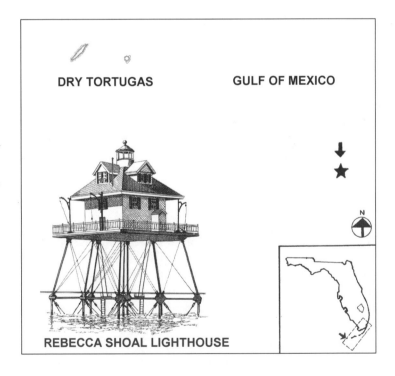

DRY TORTUGAS   GULF OF MEXICO

REBECCA SHOAL LIGHTHOUSE

DRY TORTUGAS/ TORTUGAS HARBOR

LIGHTHOUSE (OLD TOWER)

GARDEN KEY, DRY TORTUGAS, FLORIDA

By Neil Hurley

*T*ortugas is the Spanish word for turtle. It was the presence of large numbers of sea turtles and a lack of fresh water that gave this island group its name when it was discovered by Spanish explorer Ponce de León in 1513. The island group is the westernmost of the Florida Keys and has historically been a great danger to ships moving from the Gulf of Mexico to the Atlantic.

Although the British considered building a lighthouse in the Dry Tortugas in 1773, the first lighthouse was built in 1825 under American ownership. The sixty-five-foot-tall brick lighthouse and its detached keeper's dwelling were the first permanent buildings in the Dry Tortugas. The tower showed a white light from twenty-three lamps, each with a fourteen-inch reflector. The buildings were located on Garden Key, which was in the center of the island group and also had the advantage of being next to one of the best anchorages around. The lighthouse was first lighted on July 4, 1826, the fiftieth anniversary of the signing of the Declaration of Independence and the same day that Thomas Jefferson died. Ironically, the huge fort built around the lighthouse twenty years later would bear Jefferson's name.

The lighthouse's first keeper, retired Major John Flaherty, had a hard time keeping a good light and was transferred to the less remote Sand Key Light near Key West, in part due to a request from his wife to the president of the United States. The loneliness of Garden Key ended when construction of Fort Jefferson was started in 1847. The fort would eventually surround the lighthouse. Just after the Civil War, the cries of a prisoner being tortured at the fort kept the keeper's family awake all night.

The lighthouse on Garden Key was downgraded in importance after a taller light was built on nearby Loggerhead Key in 1856. By 1874, some people thought the old Garden Key Tower detracted from the appearance of the parade ground of the fort. The combined effects of years of hurricanes also made the tower unsafe. In 1876, a new lighthouse was built on the wall of Fort Jefferson, and the old tower was torn down soon after.

Today, the foundation of the 1826 Dry Tortugas Lighthouse tower remains visible inside Fort Jefferson.

Site Facts

Date of Construction: 1826
First Lighted: July 4, 1826
Tower Height (base to floor of lantern room): 65 feet
Focal Plane: 70 feet
Architect: unknown
Builder: Noah Humphries
Type of Construction: brick conical tower
Foundation Materials: brick
Construction Materials: brick with wood steps
Number of Steps: 70 (approximate)
Daymark: white tower with black lantern
Active: no
Deactivated: 1873
Original Lighting Apparatus: twenty-three lamps in fourteen-inch reflectors
Manufacturer and Date: Winslow Lewis (1826)
Other Apparatus Used: seventeen lamps in twenty-three-inch reflectors (1838), fourth-order Fresnel lens (1858)
Manufacturer and Date: Henry-LePaute (1858)
Present Optic: none

Characteristic: fixed white light

Auxiliary Historic Structures: surrounded by Fort Jefferson

National Register Listing: yes (part of Fort Jefferson National Monument)

Operating Entity: National Park Service

Tower Open to the Public: yes (base of tower only)

Lighthouse Museum: no

Gift Shop: yes (at Fort Jefferson)

Hours: 8 A.M.–5 P.M.

Handicapped Access: no

Contact: Dry Tortugas National Park, P.O. Box 6208, Key West, FL 33041; (305) 242-7700

Directions:

From Key West, boats or seaplanes provide the only access to the Dry Tortugas. Information about transportation to the park from Key West (65 miles) may be obtained from the park at (305) 242-7700 or from the Key West Chamber of Commerce, Old Mallory Square,

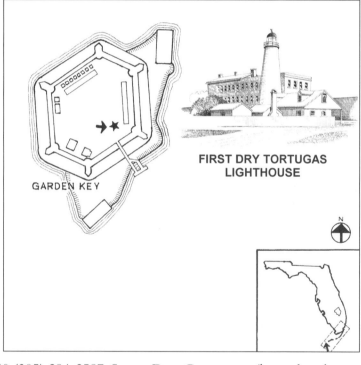

GARDEN KEY

FIRST DRY TORTUGAS LIGHTHOUSE

Key West, FL 33040 (305) 294-2587. Sunny Days Catamarans (located at the corner of Greene & Elizabeth Streets in Key West, 1-800-236-7937) has the fastest boat that goes out to the Dry Tortugas. Private boaters must be fully self-sufficient with water, fuel, and supplies. The park has no boat moorings or slips. Overnight anchorage is limited to the designated area within 1 nautical mile of Fort Jefferson.

TORTUGAS HARBOR

LIGHTHOUSE (NEW TOWER)

GARDEN KEY, DRY TORTUGAS, FLORIDA

By Neil Hurley

After the old 1826 lighthouse tower on Garden Key in the Dry Tortugas was heavily damaged in an 1873 hurricane and reported to be an unsafe eyesore, a new lighthouse tower was built on the walls of Fort Jefferson in 1874. The new tower was constructed of boilerplate iron since a brick lighthouse could cause dangerous brick fragments if hit by an enemy cannon shell. The tower has six sides and originally showed a light from a fourth-order Fresnel lens.

Since 1858, when the lighthouse on Loggerhead Key was lit, the Garden Key lighthouse was known as the Dry Tortugas Harbor light. This changed in 1883, when the tower's official name became the Tortugas Harbor light.

Around 1890, a new keeper's dwelling was built in the same location as the old one, adjacent to the parade ground inside the walls of Fort Jefferson. The fort had been abandoned by the army in 1874, but from 1889, a quarantine station and a buoy depot shared the island with the lighthouse keeper and his family. During the late 1890s, the military returned to Fort Jefferson for a short time during the Spanish-American War. The fort was abandoned again after 1910 because of damage caused by a hurricane.

The fort's value as a military post was ended in 1912. A fire started in the light-house's outhouse at around 2:30 in the morning, quickly spreading to another shed, then to the lighthouse keeper's home and a three-story brick barracks. Kitchen buildings behind the barracks also caught on fire. Only the wooden drawbridge leading into the fort was saved. The lighthouse was automated the next year and the keeper's house was never rebuilt.

The Tortugas Harbor light was discontinued as unnecessary in 1921. The tower, now maintained as part of Fort Jefferson National Monument, still stands on the walls of Fort Jefferson. While at the fort, visit the cell where Dr. Samuel Mudd was held after he was implicated in the conspiracy to assassinate Abraham Lincoln. Dr. Mudd saved numerous lives during the 1867 yellow fever epidemic and was par-doned in 1869.

⊏⊐ Site **Facts** ▬▬

Date of Construction: 1876
First Lighted: April 5, 1876
Tower Height (base to top): 25 feet
Focal Plane: 67 feet
Architect: unknown
Builders: unknown
Type of Construction: cast-iron, hexagonal pyramidal tower
Foundation Materials: brick casemate of fort
Construction Materials: boilerplate iron with wood steps
Number of Steps: 50 steps within the fort; 33 steps in the lighthouse proper
Daymark: dark brown, later black
Active: No
Deactivated: 1921
Original Lighting Apparatus: fourth-order Fresnel lens
Manufacturer and Date: Henry-LePaute (1858)
Other Apparatus Used: none
Manufacturer and Date:
Present Optic: three ordinary light bulbs
Characteristic: fixed white light
Auxiliary Historic Structures: surrounded by Fort Jefferson.
National Register Listing: yes (part of Fort Jefferson National Monument)
Operating Entity: National Park Service

Tower Open to the Public: yes (base of tower only)
Lighthouse Museum: no
Gift Shop: yes (at Fort Jefferson)
Hours: 8: 00 A.M.–5:00 P.M.
Handicapped Access: no
Contact: Dry Tortugas National Park, P.O. Box 6208, Key West, FL 33041;
(305) 242-7700

Directions:
This lighthouse is located adjacent to the Old Dry Tortugas/Tortugas Harbor
Lighthouse within Fort Jefferson. To get to the Dry Tortugas, follow the direc-
tions in the previous chapter.

GARDEN KEY

TORTUGAS HARBOR
LIGHTHOUSE

DRY TORTUGAS LIGHTHOUSE

LOGGERHEAD KEY, DRY TORTUGAS, FLORIDA

By Neil Hurley

As early as 1836, mariners complained about the lighthouse tower on Garden Key. Despite a number of shipwrecks in the intervening years, it wasn't until late 1856 that funds were approved for a new, larger lighthouse to be built closer to the most dangerous reefs on Loggerhead Key.

The new Dry Tortugas Lighthouse was first lighted on July 1, 1858. The first-order Fresnel lens was maintained by a keeper, his family, and two assistant keepers, the only residents of the mile-long island. When Benjamin Kerr, the first keeper, moved from his old job at the Tortugas Harbor Lighthouse on Garden Key, he brought his wife and two daughters with him. All was well until one of Kerr's daughters fell in love with one of the assistants. With Kerr and one of his daughters on one side and his wife, other daughter, and the two assistant keepers on the opposing side, a fight ensued. Clubs, chairs, and knives were used before Kerr and his daughter escaped to Fort Jefferson. The two assistant keepers were later removed from their posts, and Kerr and his wife separated, Mrs. Kerr moving to Key West.

Hurricane winds in 1873 caused the tower to vibrate so much that the top of the lighthouse was nearly blown off. Plans were made to replace the entire tower with a stronger, all-iron one, but temporary repairs held through another hurricane and the plan for a new tower was abandoned. A 1909 thunderstorm killed thousands of migratory birds on the key and left the newly painted lighthouse "literally plastered with brilliant feathers." A hurricane in 1910 blew windowpanes out from around the lens. After the storm, bits of wind-blown seaweed were found at the top of the tower, more than 160 feet above sea level.

From 1904 until 1939, lighthouse keepers shared Loggerhead Key with scientists from the Carnegie Marine Biological Laboratory. The lab conducted some of the first research on coral reefs and mangroves in the Western hemisphere and also took the first ever black-and-white and color underwater photographs. During World War II, the Coast Guard posted additional people at Loggerhead Key to act as coastal lookouts. One of these lookouts may have been responsible for the accidental fire that destroyed the two-story, brick keeper's dwelling in 1945.

Today, the lighthouse continues to be operated by the U.S. Coast Guard, but the buildings and island are maintained by the National Park Service as part of Dry Tortugas National Park.

▭ Site Facts ▬

Dates of Construction: 1857–1858
First Lighted: July 1, 1858
Tower Height (ground to top of lantern): 157 feet
Focal Plane: 151 feet
Architect: unknown
Builders: under supervision of engineers at Fort Jefferson
Type of Construction: brick, conical tower
Foundation Materials: brick and stone
Construction Materials: brick with granite steps; iron
Number of Steps: 204
Daymark: conical brick tower, lower half white, upper half black
Active: yes
Original Lighting Apparatus: first-order Fresnel lens
Manufacturer and Date: L. Sautter (1858)
Other Apparatus Used: second-order bivalve lens
Manufacturer and Date: Henry-LePaute (circa 1910; removed in 1984)
Present Optic: DCB 24-inch rotating beacon
Characteristic: flashing white light every twenty seconds

Auxiliary Historic Structures: former kitchen, 1926 dwelling, cisterns, attached oil house
National Register Listing: no
Operating Entities: United States Coast Guard, National Park Service
Tower Open to the Public: periodically opened by park rangers
Lighthouse Museum: no
Hours: none
Gift shop: yes (at Fort Jefferson)
Handicapped Access: no
Contact: Dry Tortugas National Park, P. O. Box 6208, Key West, FL 33041; (305) 242-7700

Directions:

This lighthouse is located about 2.5 miles west of Fort Jefferson. See section on Tortugas Harbor (Old Dry Tortugas) Lighthouse for directions to Fort Jefferson.

DRY TORTUGAS LIGHTHOUSE

SANIBEL ISLAND LIGHTHOUSE

SANIBEL, FLORIDA

By Charles LeBuff

I n 1833, a group of New York investors platted a settlement on the island known as "Sanybel." Their elaborate plan indicated the future location of a lighthouse to aid in commerce, but their hopes for long-term settlement of the island were short-lived. A harsh environment with hordes of mosquitoes, frequent hurricanes, and the threat of Indian attack during the Second Seminole War caused settlers to abandon "Sanybel" Island by 1836. By mid-century, nearby Punta Rassa, on the opposite side of San Carlos Harbor from Sanibel, became a busy cattle-shipping port. Before the Civil War, the shippers asked the Lighthouse Board to approve a lighthouse for the entrance to the harbor. Their request was denied because the board determined maritime traffic did not justify construction of a new light station. However, by the early 1870s, as many as sixteen thousand head of Florida scrub cattle left Punta Rassa on vessels bound for Cuba each year.

The small seaport at Punta Rassa continued to grow, and in 1880, the Lighthouse Board finally approved another lighthouse between the Dry Tortugas and Egmont Key. At their urging, Congress appropriated the funds necessary to construct, equip, and staff the Sanibel Island Light Station. However, obstacles delayed the station's construction. The state of Florida had been granted title to public domain lands on Sanibel Island in 1845 when it entered the Union. This included East Point (now Point Ybel), the selected construction site. Quick diplomacy on the part of the federal government resulted in Florida's agreeing to relinquish any land title claims to the island. The Sanibel Island Lighthouse Reservation was established by an executive order on December 9, 1883.

Construction of the station began in March 1884. In May, when the parts for the light tower were being delivered by schooner from New Jersey, the vessel foundered on an enormous sandbar in the Gulf of Mexico south of Point Ybel. The unique cargo sank to the bottom. Salvagers, including a hardhat diver, managed to retrieve most of the iron parts, and the construction timetable continued on schedule. When first lighted in 1884, the lamp inside the lighthouse's lantern was fueled by kerosene. Upgraded in 1923, it was retrofitted with a new burner that ignited timed releases of acetylene gas. The lighthouse was electrified in 1962.

The U.S. Coast Guard took over responsibility for lighthouses and other aids to navigation in 1939. The last of the resident keepers left the Sanibel Island Light Station ten years later. Because of major damage to the station's buildings and water supply during a 1948 hurricane, it was determined that the quarters were unsafe to be used by Coast Guard personnel. In early 1949, the light was listed as unwatched and fully automated.

In April 1949, the U. S. Fish and Wildlife Service negotiated a revocable lease with the Coast Guard and assumed responsibility for the land and structures (excluding the light tower) for the headquarters of the Sanibel National Wildlife Refuge, renamed the J. N. "Ding" Darling National Wildlife Refuge in 1967. Permanent employees of that agency resided in the lighthouse quarters and maintained the refuge office at Point Ybel until 1982. Today, the quarters are occupied by employees of the city of Sanibel. The city manages the land under a lease agreement with the Coast Guard, but the still-functioning light remains under Coast Guard jurisdiction. In 1974, the quarters and tower were listed on the National Register of Historic Places.

▭ Site Facts ▬

Date of Construction: 1884
First Lighted: August 20, 1884
Tower Height (ground to top of lantern): 112 feet
Focal Plane: 98 feet

Architect: unknown
Builders: Phoenix Ironworks, Ocean City, NJ
Type of Construction: iron skeletal tower
Foundation Materials: concrete
Construction Materials: iron pilings
Number of Steps: 101
Daymark: brown square pyramidal skeletal tower enclosing stair cylinder
Active: yes
Unmanned: 1949
Original Lighting Apparatus: third-order revolving Fresnel lens (1884–1923) (The pedestal dates from this lens.)
Manufacturer and Date: unknown
Other Apparatus Used: third-order fixed Fresnel lens (1923–1962)
Manufacturer and Date: unknown
Other Apparatus Used: Swedish 500mm drum lens (1962–1982) (on display at the Sanibel Historical Village and Museum)
Manufacturer and Date: unknown
Present Optic: 300mm lantern
Characteristic: flashing white twice every six seconds
Auxiliary Historic Structures: two elevated, wood-frame keeper's dwellings (1884); brick oil storage house (1894)
National Register Listing: yes
Operating Entity: United States Coast Guard
Tower Open to the Public: no
Lighthouse Museum: lighthouse exhibit in Burnap Cottage at the Sanibel Historical Village and Museum
Hours: Sanibel Historical Village and Museum; summer: Wednesday through Saturday, 10 A.M.–4 P.M.; winter: Wednesday through Saturday, 10 A.M.–4 P.M.; Sunday 1–4 P.M.
Gift Shop: at museum
Handicapped Access: no

Directions:

From Key West, return north on US 1. At Homestead, take the Florida Turnpike, Homestead Extension, north to I-75. Follow I-75 north towards Fort Myers and take Exit 21 to Daniels Parkway. Proceed west across US 41; here the roadway becomes Cypress Lake Drive. Turn left onto State Route 869 (Summerlin Road), pass through tollbooth ($3 per car), and cross Sanibel Causeway. At the stop sign, bear left and follow Periwinkle Way to the lighthouse. No parking is permitted on the lighthouse grounds. Two parking lots (hourly fee) are located on Point Ybel, one on the gulf side and the other on the bay side. There are restrooms and walking trails to the lighthouse.

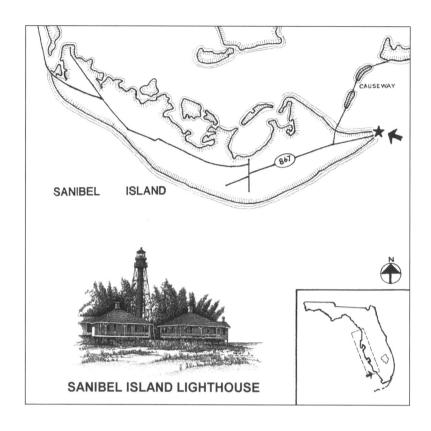

SANIBEL ISLAND LIGHTHOUSE

BOCA GRANDE
ENTRANCE REAR RANGE LIGHT

GASPARILLA ISLAND, FLORIDA

By Marilyn Hoeckel

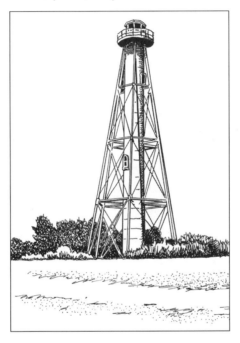

The Boca Grande Entrance Rear Range Light is one of only a handful of lighthouses that have had active service in two states. According to new research, this tower was originally built in 1881 to serve as the Delaware Breakwater Rear Range Lighthouse, north of Lewes, Delaware, and was known locally as the Green Hill Lighthouse (although no hill actually exists). This could well be correct, as a nearly identical tower was built in 1877 and still exists as the Liston Range Rear Light, near Taylor's Bridge, Delaware. The black-painted Delaware Breakwater Rear Range Lighthouse displayed a red light from its third-order lens at a focal plane of 108 feet. However, due to shoreline changes, this lighthouse was discontinued in 1918. The clockwork and lens were shipped for use on the West Coast.

In 1919, the Seventh Lighthouse District in Florida notified the district supervisor of the Delaware station that there was a need for the tower in Florida; however, funding for transporting the lighthouse to Florida and erecting it here was not then available. When some funding became available in 1921, the lighthouse tower was dismantled—each part marked and numbered for easy reassembly—and the iron tower was shipped by railroad to Miami. Again, funding problems delayed the reerection of the lighthouse, but finally, in 1927, the United States Lighthouse Service erected the skeletal, 106-foot-tall rear range light on Gasparilla Island about a mile north of the Port Boca Grande (Gasparilla Island) Lighthouse at the southern tip of the island.

The tower was painted white, and a fourth-order bivalve lens was installed and lighted in 1932. The light was never manned but was maintained by the keepers of the Port Boca Grande (Gasparilla Island) Lighthouse. It was of great commercial importance during the heyday of Port Boca Grande in the third quarter of the twentieth century, guiding ships from all over the world through the treacherous waters of the Boca Grande Navigation Channel into safe harborage inside Charlotte Harbor.

It is the rear range light that is mainly used by ships to proceed safely into Port Boca Grande. A ship's captain can tell which of the two Boca Grande lighthouses he is seeing because of the difference in the flash sequences. As a vessel proceeds in the ship's channel, heading for south Gasparilla Island, the captain sees, fixed in the water, the front range light, a twenty-foot-tall steel structure with a flashing light on top. He lines up this range light with the tall rear range light on land. By so doing, he knows he is in the middle of the channel. A drift of fifty feet either way could run his ship aground.

At this time, the future of the Boca Grande Entrance Rear Range Light is uncertain. In 1998, Florida Power and Light, the sole commercial user of Port Boca Grande, announced that by 2002 it will no longer need or use the Port Boca Grande oil terminal to receive oil shipments. In August 1999, the Coast Guard announced that it was turning the rear range light over to the General Services Administration for disposal. Perhaps a new owner will acquire the lighthouse and the land immediately surrounding it, preserving this striking tower for the future.

Site Facts

Date of Construction: 1927
First Lighted: 1932
Tower Height (from ground to top of lantern): 106 feet
Focal Plane: 105 feet
Architect: unknown
Builders: Phoenix Iron Company, Trenton, NJ
Type of Construction: iron skeletal tower
Foundation Materials: concrete

Construction Materials: iron pilings

Number of Steps: unknown

Daymark: white, hexagonal, pyramidal skeletal tower enclosing central stair cylinder

Active: yes

Original Lighting Apparatus: third-order red Fresnel lens (Delaware, 1881–1918)

Manufacturer and Date: unknown

Other Apparatus Used: fourth-order bivalve Fresnel lens (Florida, 1932)

Manufacturer and Date: unknown

Modern Optics: FA-251 rotating lantern

Present Optic: FA-251 rotating lantern

Characteristic: fixed red light (originally); flashing white every six seconds (currently)

Auxiliary Historic Structures: none

National Register Listing: no

Operating Entity: United States Coast Guard

Tower Open to the Public: no   **Lighthouse Museum:** no

Hours: none

Gift Shop: no   **Handicapped Access:** no

Directions:

From the Sanibel Island Lighthouse, return to I-75. Take I-75 north and get off at Exit 31 (Veteran's Boulevard) to Murdock. Cross over State Route 41; you are now on State Route 776. Cross over the Myakka River to State Route 771; turn left at the sign for Boca Grande. Go about 10 miles to the Boca Grande Causeway and turn left. There is a $3.20 toll to get onto the island. Head south on Gasparilla Road to a four-way stop sign. Turn right and then left onto Gulf Boulevard. The Boca Grande Entrance Rear Range Light is on the beach to your right, just south of First Street. Although it is not open to the public, you can park in the state parking lot and take pictures.

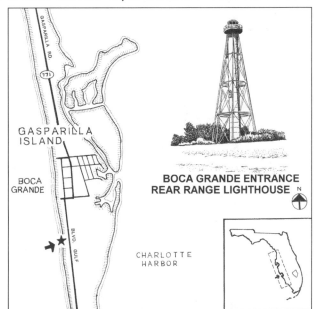

BOCA GRANDE ENTRANCE REAR RANGE LIGHTHOUSE N

PORT BOCA GRANDE (GASPARILLA ISLAND) LIGHTHOUSE

GASPARILLA ISLAND, FLORIDA

By Marilyn Hoeckel

The Port Boca Grande Lighthouse, originally called the Gasparilla Island Light Station, was built in 1890 at the southern tip of Gasparilla Island to mark the entry into Charlotte Harbor from the Gulf of Mexico. From its perch on deep-water Boca Grande Pass, it first saw service guiding cattle ships going from Charlotte Harbor to Cuba. In 1912, Port Boca Grande, served by a railroad to the phosphate mines in Polk County, opened as a state-of-the-art international shipping facility. For the next sixty-seven years, the lighthouse guided oceangoing ships from more than twenty countries traveling to Boca Grande to load phosphate, a valuable commodity worldwide for making fertilizer.

The lighthouse is the oldest building on Gasparilla Island. The assistant light-keeper's house, of nearly identical style but without the lantern tower, was built next door at the same time. The restored buildings are today the centerpiece of Gasparilla Island State Recreation Area.

The lighthouse, a one-story wooden dwelling on iron pilings with a black octagonal lantern on top, has survived seven hurricanes, a fire that burned down a washhouse just a few feet away, and severe beach erosion. In the early years, lighthouse keepers, living a lonely life on the isolated barrier island, played host to millionaires like John D. Rockefeller and John Jacob Astor, who came to Boca Grande Pass in their yachts to fish for the mighty tarpon. During World War II, the light guided hundreds of grateful U.S. and Allied cargo ships, seeking refuge from German submarines lurking off the coast, into safe harborage.

In 1956, the lighthouse was automated and unmanned, and in 1966, the light was removed and the Coast Guard turned the building over to the General Services Administration for disposal. Thirteen acres of land and ownership of the dilapidated building—leaning at an angle, its stairs rotted away and gulf waters lapping at it due to beach erosion—were transferred to Lee County in 1972. The local power company helped the lighthouse survive by pumping sand around the structure and by building two rock groins along the new shoreline.

The lighthouse was placed on the National Register of Historic Places in 1980, and in 1985–86, island citizens, under the leadership of the Gasparilla Island Conservation and Improvement Association, restored the lighthouse with help from the Florida Bureau of Historic Preservation. A 375mm drum lens was installed, and the lighthouse was recommissioned by the Coast Guard on November 21, 1986. The state of Florida took over ownership in 1988, and in 1999, the lighthouse opened to the public as the Boca Grande Lighthouse Museum. The museum was created and is operated by the Barrier Island Parks Society, a volunteer organization for the park. The Coast Guard maintains the light, which continues to mark the southern tip of Gasparilla Island as it has done since 1890.

The Port Boca Grande Lighthouse came close to total destruction. It is open to the public today through the remarkable efforts of government, private citizens, and businesses working together to preserve an important piece of Florida's history.

Site Facts

Date of Construction: 1890
First Lighted: December 31, 1890
Tower Height: 44 feet
Focal Plane: 41 feet
Architect: unknown
Builders: unknown
Type of Construction: house-style lighthouse on iron pilings
Foundation Materials: iron pilings
Construction Materials: wood and iron
Number of Steps (ground to lantern room): 60

Daymark: white frame dwelling with green shutters and a black lantern tower
Active: yes
Deactivated: 1966–1986
Original Lighting Apparatus: third-and-a-half-order revolving Fresnel lens
Manufacturer and Date: unknown
Present Optic: 300mm drum lens
Characteristic: occulting white light every four seconds
Auxiliary Historic Structures: assistant keeper's house, two cisterns, generator shed,
    replica boardwalk
National Register Listing: yes
Operating Entity: Florida State Park Service
Tower Open to the Public: no
Lighthouse Museum: yes
Hours: Wednesday–Sunday, 10 A.M.–4 P.M.; closed August and major holidays
Gift Shop: yes
Handicapped Access: yes
Contact: Barrier Island Parks Society, P.O. Box 637, Boca Grande, FL 33921; (941) 697-
    7750; fax (941) 697-2822; e-mail: hoeckel@gls3c.com

Directions:

From the Boca
Grande Entrance
Rear Range Light,
continue south on
Gulf Boulevard.
Follow signs for
the state park and
Lighthouse
Museum at the
southern tip of the
island. There is a
$2 fee to enter the
state park.

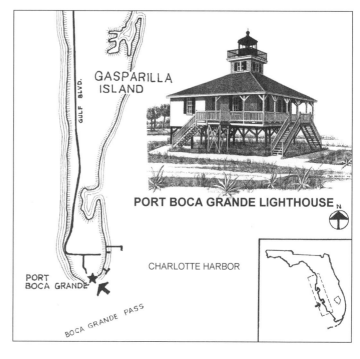

CHARLOTTE HARBOR LIGHTHOUSE
(Lighthouse Site Only)

NEAR PUNTA GORDA, FLORIDA

By Neil Hurley

harlotte Harbor is a large bay on Florida's west coast. It was described in the 1880s as "possessing the greater natural advantages than any other (harbor) on the Gulf coast, and has been pronounced by competent authority to be the best harbor between Port Royal and Pensacola." Despite this grand description, the shallow depths of the inner part of the bay prevented development of a port for large seagoing ships.

When a railroad line came to nearby Punta Gorda, a town at the head of the bay in the mid-1880s, the town gained importance as a cattle-shipping port. With $35,000 appropriated by Congress in 1889, a small lighthouse was built in water nine feet deep near the center of the bay in 1890. It marked a turning point in the twelve-foot-deep channel.

This lighthouse, which was built at the same time as the similar Gasparilla Island Lighthouse nearby, was a wooden dwelling on iron piles with the lantern on top.

The lighthouse was painted white and had green shutters, a red roof, and a black lantern. Three rooms were in the lower story of the house, and two rooms were on the second floor. A keeper and one assistant manned the lighthouse. Originally, a red fixed light was displayed, but by 1918, the light was a flashing white one. Since it was located southeast of Cape Haze, this lighthouse was sometimes also called the Cape Haze Lighthouse in the early days

When another railroad line reached the deep-water port at the south tip of Gasparilla Island in 1906, Charlotte Harbor's days as an important port were numbered. By 1911, the lighthouse was converted to acetylene gas, and it was unmanned before 1918. The lighthouse remained active until the early 1930s. In 1943, it was described as "badly deteriorated and unsightly from lack of proper maintenance." The same year, the lighthouse was torn down and replaced with an iron skeletal tower. Today, Charlotte Harbor Light 6, a single pile structure with red triangular dayboards, stands watch at the lighthouse's former location.

▭ Site Facts ▬

Date of Construction: 1890
First Lighted: 1890
Tower Height (sea bottom to top of lantern): 50 feet (approximate)
Focal Plane: 36 feet
Architect: unknown
Builders: unknown
Type of Construction: house-style lighthouse on iron pilings
Foundation Materials: iron piles
Construction Materials: wood and iron
Number of Steps: unknown
Daymark: white house with green shutters, red roof, and black lantern
Active: no
Deactivated: before 1935
Original Lighting Apparatus: fifth-order fixed, red Fresnel lens
Manufacturer and Date: unknown
Other Apparatus Used: fifth-order white revolving Fresnel lens
Manufacturer and Date: unknown
Present Optic: solar-powered 155mm lens
Characteristic: fixed red light (originally); flashing white every second (later); none (currently)
Auxiliary Historic Structures: none
National Register Listing: no
Operating Entity: United States Coast Guard
Tower Open to the Public: historic tower is no longer present

Lighthouse Museum: no
Hours: none
Gift Shop: no
Handicapped Access: no

Directions:

This lighthouse site can be reached only by boat and cannot be seen from any nearby access road. The present structure, Charlotte Harbor Light 6, is located in position 26°45'35" 82°06'29", 2.5 miles southeast by east from Cape Haze and about 8.5 miles from the south end of Gasparilla Island. For those who wish to visit the site of this vanished lighthouse, a free public boat ramp is located at the north end of the Boca Grande causeway, and there are at least two boat rental establishments in Boca Grande.

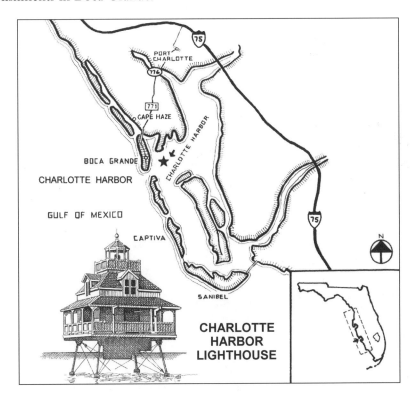

CHARLOTTE HARBOR LIGHTHOUSE

EGMONT KEY LIGHTHOUSE

NEAR ST. PETERSBURG, FLORIDA

By Richard Johnson

After Spain ceded Florida to the United States in 1821, commerce along the gulf coast increased rapidly. Although Tampa Bay would not be a significant port for some years, a lighthouse was requested as early as 1833 to aid vessels running along the coast from Key West to Pensacola. In 1838, Capt. Lawrence Rousseau, during a survey of all aids to navigation in the gulf, recommended the construction of a lighthouse at Egmont Key. Congress appropriated $7,580, and a lighthouse and keeper's house were built on the north end of the island. The lighthouse was lighted in May 1848. At the time, it was the only lighthouse between St. Marks and Key West. On September 25, a severe hurricane damaged the tower and keeper's house, and despite various repairs, it was necessary to replace the original tower. The new lighthouse, built to "withstand any storm," was completed at a cost of $16,000 in 1858 and is still in use today.

Early in the Civil War, keeper George Richards removed the lens and most of the lighthouse supplies to Tampa to keep them out of Union hands. Starting in July 1861, the island was occupied by Union forces and served as a base of operations for the East Gulf Blockading Squadron. The light was relighted in June 1866.

In 1872, a buoy depot was established at Egmont Key, and by 1889, all of the buoys used between Key West and St. Marks were repaired, serviced, and painted at the Egmont Key depot. Between 1898 and 1923, the lighthouse keepers shared Egmont Key with Fort Dade, one of the Army's primary coastal defense installations in the Gulf of Mexico. Extensive ruins of Fort Dade can still be observed on the island.

In 1944, because of water damage to the lantern room, the lantern was removed, the tower was shortened to seventy feet, and an electric lamp was put in place for the first time. In 1978, Egmont Key was listed on the National Register of Historic Places. In 1989, the Egmont Key Lighthouse was the last lighthouse in Florida to be completely automated and unmanned. Today, Egmont Key is co-managed by the Florida Park Service and the U.S. Fish and Wildlife Service. The Egmont Key Alliance, a civilian support group, and other lighthouse enthusiasts hope someday to restore the lantern on this lighthouse. A gift shop is currently being planned.

Site Facts

Dates of Construction: 1847–1848; 1857–1858

First Lighted: May 1848; 1858

Tower Height: 81 feet (as built); 76 feet (after modification during the 1940s)

Architect: Augustus Angstrom

Builders: unknown

Type of Construction: masonry conical tower

Construction Materials: brick, concrete, and iron

Number of Steps (ground to lantern room): 99

Daymark: white conical tower (no lantern)

Active: yes

Original Lighting Apparatus: third-order fixed Fresnel lens

Manufacturer and Date: Henry-LePaute (1858)

Other Apparatus: unknown

Modern Optics: one DCB-236 electric rotating beacon

Present Optic: DCB-24 electric rotating beacon

Characteristic: fixed white light (originally); flashing white every fifteen seconds (currently)

Auxiliary Historic Structures: radio and generator building, oil storage house, modern staff quarters

National Register Listing: yes (as part of Egmont Key)

Operating Entities: United States Coast Guard and Florida Park Service
Tower Open to the Public: grounds open daily; base of tower open occasionally
Lighthouse Museum: no
Hours: varied
Gift Shop: no
Handicapped Access: by arrangement
Contact: Park Manager, Egmont Key State Park, 4905 34th Street South #5000, St. Petersburg, FL 33711; (727) 893-2627; e-mail: egmontkey@juno.com

Directions:

From Gasparilla Island, return to I-75. Head north; after passing through Bradenton, take the exit to I-275 and the Sunshine Skyway Bridge. After crossing the bridge ($1 toll) and reaching St. Petersburg, take Exit 4 and go west on the Pinellas Bayway State Route 682 (toll), then south on Pinellas Bayway State Route 679 (toll) to Fort DeSoto Park. Once in the park, go west to the gun emplacements at Fort DeSoto or to the Gulf Fishing Pier for the best view. The tower may also be viewed from the southwest area of Fort DeSoto Park.

Egmont Key is accessible only by boat. There are various commercial excursion boats with regularly scheduled passenger service available in the Tampa Bay area. There are no docking facilities; privately owned boats may anchor near the key. There are limited restrooms and no drinking water or other provisions available. Captain Bill's Destiny Charters, Inc., located on the Pinellas Bayway at the Tierra Verde Hi and Dry Marina, provides charter service to Egmont Key. Charters are reasonably priced and include snorkeling gear for those interested.

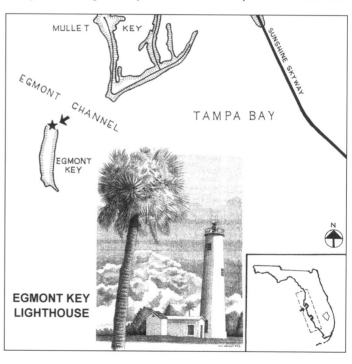

EGMONT KEY
LIGHTHOUSE

ANCLOTE KEYS
LIGHTHOUSE

ANCLOTE KEY, OFF THE COAST OF
TARPON SPRINGS, FLORIDA

By Janet and Scott Keeler

The Anclote Keys Lighthouse was built in 1887 by order of then-president Grover Cleveland as one of a chain of sentinels built on Florida's gulf coast in the 1880s. It cost the U.S. Lighthouse Service $35,000 to build the cast-iron skeletal structure as part of a federal coastline defense program.

What today is a sleepy barrier island—due to the deactivation of the lighthouse in 1985—was once the welcome wagon for dignitaries, tourists, mariners, and townsfolk who gathered under the Florida long-leaf pine and sabal palms for family socials. While the island's beauty was a natural draw, the lighthouse made human habitation on the 188-acre island possible.

On September 15, 1887, a kerosene lamp lighted the third-order Fresnel lens and started the boom times for Tarpon Springs. The city, incorporated that same year, began to build hotels to accommodate tourists. The lighthouse also facilitated the

117

growth of the city's sponge industry, for which Tarpon Springs is still known.

Up until the Anclote Keys Lighthouse was constructed, nearly all the sponge used in the United States was imported from the islands of the eastern Mediterranean. There had been a sponge industry in the Bahamas and in Key West, Florida, since the 1840s. Schooners from Apalachicola, Florida, harvesting just a few miles off Anclote Key, were forced to haul their bounty south to Key West to sell. The lighthouse changed that: once it lighted the way from the sea up the Anclote River to safe haven in Tarpon Springs, Greek divers and their families flocked to the new American city. From 1907 to 1972, the Tarpon Springs Sponge Exchange was the largest such market in the United States. Though the industry has slowed from its heyday, Tarpon Springs continues to draw tourists, who eat Greek food such as gyros and souvlaki and almost always return home with a sponge.

Originally, two families lived on the island to tend the light. During the Spanish-American War in the late 1890s, one keeper procured a small cannon for self-defense. He never had to use it. Another keeper kept pigs on the island, letting them roam free. They were stolen by the crew of a passing boat.

In the years since the lighthouse was deactivated, both keeper's quarters have been burned to the ground by arsonists, the glass lantern panels have been shattered by gunfire, and graffiti artists have defaced the structure. The untended lighthouse has been further ravaged by the elements; the cast-iron skeleton is badly rusted. Though the steps to the top are still intact, the public is prohibited from climbing them for safety reasons.

There is good news for this once-proud, now-tattered lighthouse. A concerned group of west coast Florida residents have formed the Relight the Light Committee and have earned the lighthouse a place on the National Register of Historic Places. The state of Florida now owns the lighthouse, and the Florida legislature has already approved some funds for the renovation project. More is needed to refurbish the existing tower and to build a museum and a permanent home for state park rangers.

▭ Site Facts ▬

Date of Construction: 1887
First Lighted: September 15, 1887
Tower Height (ground to top of lantern): 96 feet
Focal Plane: 84 feet
Architect: unknown
Builders: unknown (under the supervision of U.S. Lighthouse Service engineers)
Type of Construction: iron, skeletal tower
Foundation Materials: cement
Construction Materials: iron
Number of Steps (ground to lantern room): 138 (approximate)

Daymark: rust-colored, square, pyramidal skeletal tower with black top (originally all black)

Active: no   **Deactivated:** 1985

Original Lighting Apparatus: third-order revolving Fresnel lens

Manufacturer and Date: Henry-LePaute (date unknown)

Other Apparatus Used: unknown

Manufacturer and Date: unknown

Modern Optics: 250-watt electric lamp powered by fifty-six batteries (1960s)

Present Optic: none

Characteristic: flashing white every five seconds (originally)

Auxiliary Historic Structures: oil house and cistern

National Register Listing: yes

Operating Entity: state of Florida (Gulf Islands GEO Park)

Tower Open to the Public: no   **Lighthouse Museum:** no

Hours: none

Gift Shop: no   **Handicapped Access:** no

Contact: Park Manager, Gulf Islands GEO Park, # 1 Causeway Drive, Dunedin, FL 34698; (727) 469-5942

Directions:

From the view of Egmont Key Lighthouse at Fort DeSoto Park, return to US 19 and head north through St. Petersburg and Clearwater. At State Route 582 (Keystone Road), turn left (west) into Tarpon Springs. Located on the southern end of the island, at the mouth of the Anclote River, the Anclote Keys Lighthouse is less than 3 miles from the mainland and is accessible only by boat. Rental boats are available in Tarpon Springs, and excursions to the island are

offered by Island Wind Tours. These leave from Anclote River Park, 1119 Baillie's Bluff Road, Holiday. For information, call (813) 934-0606. To launch your own boat, take US 19A north to State Route 76 (Anclote Boulevard) and go west to the Anclote Key Park boat ramp. Check with park rangers at the Gulf Islands GEO Park (Honeymoon Island State Park) at (727) 469-5942 regarding rules and regulations for the Anclote Keys Lighthouse site.

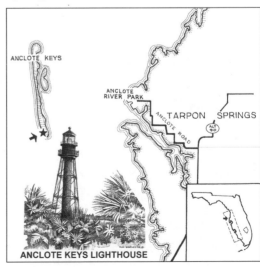

ANCLOTE KEYS LIGHTHOUSE

CEDAR KEYS LIGHTHOUSE

SEAHORSE KEY, NEAR CEDAR KEY, FLORIDA

By Elinor De Wire

Three miles from the town of Cedar Key, between the estuaries of the Suwannee and Waccasassa Rivers, is Seahorse Key, a tiny green sequin on the dark blue dress of the vast Gulf of Mexico. Though small and remote, the key has been important to navigation since 1854, when the government built the Cedar Keys Lighthouse as a beacon for freighters hauling the area's lumber and oysters.

The site chosen for the lighthouse was a large sand dune fifty-two feet above sea level. The station included a low house with a twenty-eight-foot brick tower rising from its roof. A fourth-order fixed light visible for fifteen miles completed the beacon. The architect and builder was Lt. George Gordon Meade of the Topographical Engineer Corps, well known for his work on the Florida reef, building iron screw-pile lighthouses, and for the handsome Jupiter Inlet Lighthouse, also under construction at this time. His frugal design for the lighthouse on Seahorse Key came in at a modest $12,000, which made it one of Florida's less costly light towers.

As with many other Southern sentinels, the lighthouse saw travail and change during the Civil War. It was darkened in 1861 by Confederate troops, who stormed the islet, dismantled the lens, and occupied the station as quarters. A Union gunboat captured them a short time later and used the lighthouse as a prison until the end of the war. The beacon was relighted in 1866 and enjoyed several years of vital service after the completion of Florida's cross-state railroad, which carried goods from the area to important ports on the East Coast.

By the turn of the century, lumber and fishing industries in the area had begun to decline. Big freighters no longer plied the waters here, and fishermen in their small boats relied more on small post beacons than harbor and seacoast lights. In addition, the Cedar Keys Lighthouse was becoming more difficult to see because of stands of trees on the key and its neighboring islets. In 1915, the lighthouse was abandoned.

The structure served as a private residence, whose owner added the wooden wings, until 1936, when the Cedar Keys National Wildlife Refuge was created, mainly to protect Florida's endangered nesting birds. Though the beacon was not relighted, the lighthouse became a staging point for various wildlife studies in the area. In 1953, the University of Florida established a marine laboratory in the lighthouse. Since that time, it has served as a beacon of learning for the many students and scientists whose projects add to our knowledge of Florida's natural environment.

Seahorse Key is accessible only by boat, but the history of the area and of the lighthouse is available on the mainland as part of the collection of Cedar Key State Museum (off State Road 24) and at the Cedar Key Historical Museum.

Site Facts

Date of Construction: 1854
First Lighted: August 1, 1854
Tower Height (ground to top of lantern): 33 feet
Focal Plane: 75 feet
Architect: Lt. George Gordon Meade
Builder: Lt. George Gordon Meade
Type of Construction: masonry
Foundation Materials: brick
Construction Materials: brick and iron
Number of Steps (ground to lantern room): 35
Daymark: white house-style structure with white lantern
Active: no
Deactivated: 1915
Original Lighting Apparatus: fourth-order Fresnel lens

Manufacturer and Date: Henry-LePaute (1854)

Other Apparatus Used: none

Manufacturer and Date: none

Modern Optics: none

Present Optic: none

Characteristic: fixed white light (originally)

Auxiliary Historic Structures: frame additions added to original brick structure, water tank, cistern, and oil storage house

National Register Listing: yes (part of Cedar Keys Historic and Archaeological District)

Operating Entity: University of Florida Marine Laboratory

Tower Open to the Public: no, except during special open house weekends

Lighthouse Museum: two museums in Cedar Key, the Cedar Key Historical Society Museum and the Cedar Key State Museum, have displays on the history of the lighthouse

Hours: during special open house weekends

Gift Shop: no

Handicapped Access: no

Contact: Lower Suwannee and Cedar Keys National Wildlife Refuge, 16450 NW 31 Place, Chiefland, FL 32626; (352) 493-0238

Directions:

From Tarpon Springs, return to US 19/98. Head north to State Route 24 and go west. Drive about 20 miles into the town of Cedar Key. The lighthouse is about 3 miles southwest of the town. It cannot be seen from the town, and the grounds are not open to the public. Contact the Lower Suwannee and Cedar Keys National Wildlife Refuge for information about the lighthouse. Several boat charters and boat ramps are available in Cedar Key for transportation to Seahorse Key.

ST. MARKS LIGHTHOUSE

NEAR ST. MARKS, FLORIDA

By Elinor De Wire

The Spanish established Fort San Marcos de Apalachee in 1679 near what is today the St. Marks National Wildlife Refuge. The area was visited by several Spanish explorers and flew both Spanish and English flags before becoming a territory of the United States in 1821.

Construction of a lighthouse was begun in 1828 on the east side of the entrance to the St. Marks River. The builders, Benjamin Beal and Jairus Thayer, did such poor work that the tower was rejected. A second, sturdier sentinel was built by Calvin Knowlton and went into service in 1830, with Samuel Crosby as the first keeper. Shortly thereafter, erosion threatened to undermine the lighthouse. Storms battered it during hurricane season, and the site was wholly exposed to the constant gnawing of waves. In 1842, the government opted to tear down the existing tower and build a new one.

During the Second Seminole War, keeper Crosby requested protection but was inexplicably denied both a guard and a boat for escape. Fortunately, the beacon went unharmed. Storms became a greater concern. The hurricane of September 1843 destroyed the keeper's house and sent keeper J. P. Mungerford and his family into the tower for refuge. Following the storm, a new dwelling was built, along with a seawall to protect the station.

A decade of quiet followed, during which the station's first woman keeper, Ann Dudley, served. Then, in March 1865, Confederates blockaded Apalachee Bay and attempted to blow up the lighthouse but succeeded only in damaging an eight-foot section of its lower walls. It was repaired immediately following the Civil War and was returned to service on January 8, 1867. Later, the tower was extended and a new lantern was installed.

In 1931, the St. Marks National Wildlife Refuge was established to protect local natural animals such as alligators, Canada geese, and Southern bald eagles. The eighty-foot St. Marks Lighthouse was included in the preserve. The Gresham family, with eight children and the longest tenure as keepers, cared for the beacon until 1957, when it was automated. Still maintained as an active aid by the Coast Guard, St. Marks Lighthouse is listed on the National Register of Historic Places. This lighthouse will be completely restored in the near future, turned over to the St. Marks National Wildlife Refuge, and opened to the public. A museum and gift shop are planned.

▭ Site Facts ▬

Dates of Construction: 1829–1830, 1842
First Lighted: 1831, 1842
Tower Height (ground to top of lantern): 88 feet
Focal Plane: 82 feet
Architect: Winslow Lewis
Builders: Benjamin Beal and Jairus Thayer (first tower); Calvin Knowlton (second and third towers)
Type of Construction: masonry
Foundation Materials: limestone blocks
Construction Materials: brick and iron
Number of Steps (ground to lantern room): 80
Daymark: whitewashed conical brick tower with black lantern
Active: yes
Original Lighting Apparatus: fifteen Lewis Argand lamps with fourteen-inch reflectors
Manufacturer and Date: Winslow Lewis (1831)
Other Apparatus Used: fourth-order fixed Fresnel lens
Manufacturer and Date: Henry-LePaute (1867)
Modern Optics: none

Present Optic: fourth-order fixed Fresnel lens (1867)

Characteristic: occulting white light every four seconds (electric flasher)

Auxiliary Historic Structures: attached 1871 keeper's dwelling

National Register Listing: yes

Operating Entity: United States Coast Guard and St. Marks National Wildlife Refuge

Tower Open to the Public: on special occasions (may be open regularly in 2002)

Lighthouse Museum: no

Hours: grounds open during National Wildlife Refuge hours

Gift Shop: no

Handicapped Access: no

Contact: Manager, St. Marks National Wildlife Refuge, P.O. Box 68, St. Marks, FL 32355; (850) 925-6121; fax (850) 925-6930; e-mail: r4rw_fl.smk@mail.fws.gov; websites: http://www.nettally.com/biernack/st.markslighthouse/stmarks.htm; http://cityofstmarks.cimplenet.com

Directions:

From the town of Cedar Key, return to US 19/98. Go north and then, in Perry, continue to follow US 98 west to County Route 59 at the entrance to the St. Marks National Wildlife Refuge, just east of Newport, Florida. There is a fee to enter the National Wildlife Refuge. Follow County Route 59 through the National Wildlife Refuge to its end at the lighthouse (about 10 miles).

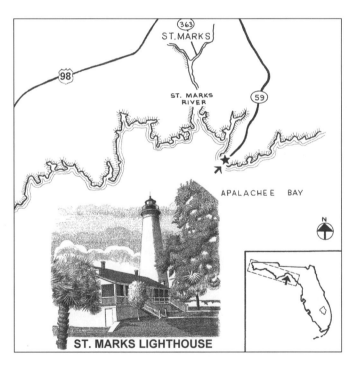

ST. MARKS LIGHTHOUSE

DOG ISLAND
LIGHTHOUSE
(Lighthouse Site Only)

NEAR CARRABELLE, FLORIDA

By Neil Hurley

The merchants and mariners of St. Marks petitioned Congress for a lighthouse on South Cape Promontory (now known as Lighthouse Point) in 1834 to mark a shoal "on which disasters are of frequent occurrence." Lighthouse authorities recommended the light be placed on the east end of St. George Island, and a compromise was eventually reached to build a lighthouse on the west end of Dog Island in 1838. As the Second Seminole War was then raging in Florida, three companies of the Sixth United States Infantry were stationed on the island to protect the lighthouse builders.

The contract called for a round, fifty-foot-tall brick tower with stone steps, a brick dwelling, a kitchen, and a privy. Winslow Lewis of Boston was the contractor, and Jacob D. Meyers, who later became the first lighthouse keeper, was appointed to superintend the lighthouse's construction. The white tower showed a flashing light from fourteen lamps in sixteen-inch reflectors.

An October 1842 hurricane destroyed the dwelling and badly damaged the top of the tower. An 1851 storm swept away the door of the lighthouse tower, reportedly killed five people, and created a new channel through the island. The lighthouse tower was destroyed, and a new tower was built the following year. During the Civil War, Confederate officials ordered the lens (a fourth-order Fresnel lens was installed in 1856) removed for safekeeping. Confederates blamed Union troops for burning the keeper's dwelling and shooting holes through the lantern. The light was finally relighted in 1866.

Beach erosion undermined the tower until, in 1872, it leaned one foot from the perpendicular. The lens was removed to a platform on the keeper's dwelling, which, because of its location farther back from the beach and its iron-pile foundation, was considered safer. Unfortunately, the Great Storm of 1873 destroyed both the tower and dwelling. Apparently the keeper and his assistant escaped unharmed. The lighthouse was never reestablished.

Today, there are no known remains of this lighthouse, although islanders say that there is a pile of bricks out in the gulf, not far from shore, and that bricks from the old lighthouse occasionally wash ashore.

Site Facts

Dates of Construction: 1838–1839
First Lighted: 1839
Tower Height (base to top of lantern): 44 feet
Focal Plane: 48 feet
Architect: Winslow Lewis
Builders: Winslow Lewis (contractor); Jacob D. Meyers (construction supervisor)
Type of Construction: brick conical tower
Foundation Materials: brick
Construction Materials: brick and iron
Number of Steps: unknown
Daymark: white conical tower with black lantern
Active: no
Deactivated: after storm of September 18–19, 1873
Original Lighting Apparatus: fourteen lamps in sixteen-inch reflectors
Manufacturer and Date: Winslow Lewis (1839)
Other Apparatus Used: revolving fourth-order Fresnel lens (1856)
Manufacturer and Date: Henry-LePaute (1855)
Modern Optics: none
Present Optics: none
Characteristic: flashing white once every minute (originally)

Auxiliary Historic Structures: none
National Register Listing: no
Operating Entity: none
Tower Open to the Public: historic tower is no longer present
Lighthouse Museum: no
Hours: none
Gift Shop: no
Handicapped Access: no

Directions:

From the St. Marks Lighthouse, return to US 98. Turn left (west) and follow US 98 all the way to Carrabelle. At Marine Street, turn left (south) to the Dog Island Ferry. Dog Island, located 3.5 miles south-southeast of Carrabelle, is not connected to the mainland by roads. The public ferry service is aboard the *Ruby B.* from Carrabelle (daily except Tuesdays and Wednesdays), and the island has a small grass airstrip. Most of Dog Island is owned by the Nature Conservancy, and there are about 130 homes there and only one road. There are no known visible remains of this lighthouse.

DOG ISLAND LIGHTHOUSE

CROOKED RIVER
LIGHTHOUSE

NEAR CARRABELLE, FLORIDA

By Barbara Revell

The East Pass between Dog and St. George Islands is one of the major inlets into St. George Sound and the port of Apalachicola. Originally, this pass was marked for navigation by the Dog Island Lighthouse, which was erected in 1839 and rebuilt in 1843 and 1852. This last tower washed away in a hurricane in 1873. With commerce in the area diminished by the Civil War, the Lighthouse Board decided not to rebuild a lighthouse on Dog Island.

Depletion of Northern forests, however, ushered in a resurgence of the local economy in the late 1880s as a new lumber industry took hold. With increased trade now beginning to pour forth from the new booming port, which would be named Carrabelle in 1897, a new lighthouse was needed. Petitions from local residents and reports from Congressional committees favored the project, and, in 1889, $40,000 was appropriated for the construction of a new lighthouse on Dog Island. In the meantime, the Lighthouse Board had decided to build a new tower on the mainland and asked that the appropriation be used for construction at that site.

Difficulties in settling the title to the land, followed by a fire that destroyed the land documents, caused the actual construction to be delayed until January 1895. The square, skeletal Crooked River Lighthouse was finally completed in August and first lighted on October 28, 1895. It contained a fourth-order Fresnel lens, which flashed from a focal plane height of 115 feet above the sea. In 1902, to give the lighthouse better contrast against the darkness of the surrounding forest, it was painted with its present color pattern—its lower half white, its upper half dark red.

Although of great importance to area commerce, this lighthouse was considered in need of only a principal keeper and one assistant. When one had to leave for an extended period—such as when the assistant keeper had to tend his seriously ill wife in Carrabelle in 1897—the other keeper had to assume all the duties.

Carrabelle was expected to develop into a major timber-exporting city, but the growth of Apalachicola to the west and a decline in the lumber industry slowed its planned growth, and only a relatively small city remained near the lighthouse. During World War II, when Camp Gordon Johnson was constructed nearby to train recruits for amphibious assault landings, the importance of the lighthouse as an aid to navigation increased. To avoid the German submarine threat off the coast of Florida, a gasoline pipeline and terminal were built in Franklin County to transport gasoline to Jacksonville. The lighthouse helped guide numerous gasoline barges into Carrabelle for the war effort. After the war, the pipeline and the training camp were dismantled, and the people of Carrabelle returned to fishing and some lumbering for survival.

The lighthouse remained to mark the east end of the north gulf coast's Intracoastal Waterway. Vessels coming west and north along Florida's west coast have to pass over two hundred miles of open gulf waters from Tarpon Springs before reaching this shelter of an inland waterway. The Crooked River Lighthouse showed them the way.

The Crooked River Lighthouse was decommissioned on August 23, 1995, and its future looked dismal. However, in 1999, the Carrabelle Lighthouse Association was founded to seek ways to preserve this important landmark of the area's maritime heritage. In 2000, the General Services Administration turned the lighthouse over to the city of Carrabelle, which has leased the lighthouse to be restored and operated as a historic site by the Carrabelle Lighthouse Association. The group plans to reopen the lighthouse, along with a museum and gift shop, to the public. What is now believed to be the original Fresnel lens from this lighthouse has recently been found in the Coast Guard district office in New Orleans.

⊏⊐ Site Facts ▬

Date of Construction: 1895
First Lighted: October 28, 1895
Tower Height (ground to top of lantern): 103 feet
Focal Plane: 115 feet
Architect: unknown
Builders: unknown
Type of Construction: steel skeletal tower
Foundation Materials: cement
Construction Materials: iron
Number of Steps (ground to lantern room): 138
Daymark: square, pyramidal, skeletal tower; lower half white, upper half dark red with a black lantern
Active: no
Deactivated: May 24, 1994
Original Lighting Apparatus: fourth-order open bivalve revolving lens
Manufacturer and Date: Henry-LePaute (1894)
Other Apparatus Used: none
Manufacturer and Date: none
Modern Optics: 190mm rotating lantern
Present Optic: none
Characteristic: two-group flashing white, flashes every twelve and a half seconds
Auxiliary Historic Structures: none on site; keeper's dwellings were moved; one still exists about two miles west
National Register Listing: yes
Operating Entity: Carrabelle Lighthouse Association
Tower Open to the Public: no
Lighthouse Museum: planned
Hours: none
Gift Shop: no
Handicapped Access: no
Contact: Carrabelle Lighthouse Association, P.O. Box 373, Carrabelle, FL 32322; (850) 697-2054; e-mail:benbar7@aol.com

Directions:

From the Dog Island Ferry in Carrabelle, return to US 98 and turn left (west) through Carrabelle. About 2 miles after crossing the Carrabelle River, look for the lighthouse high in the trees on the right. A rough dirt road will take you up to the lighthouse.

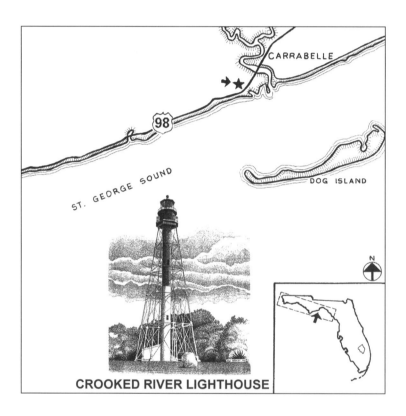

CROOKED RIVER LIGHTHOUSE

CAPE ST. GEORGE LIGHTHOUSE

LITTLE ST. GEORGE ISLAND, NEAR APALACHICOLA, FLORIDA

By John Lee

see a lighthouse!"

Few statements send photographers reaching for their camera bags and artists reaching for their sketchpads faster than this one. Lighthouses have come to symbolize the romance and excitement of a bygone era, the time of sailing ships and bold adventure.

The Cape St. George Lighthouse, built in 1852, is the third lighthouse erected on St. George Island. An earlier light was built at West Pass in 1833, but many mariners traveling from the east could not see the light until they were in danger-ously shallow water, so the lighthouse was removed. The second light was built in 1847 on Cape St. George itself. Destructive winds and seas felled it in 1851. The present lighthouse was built 250 yards inland; its first keeper was William Austin.

Although the architect is unknown, the builder was Edward Bowden of Franklin County. Bowden reused two-thirds of the bricks from the 1847 lighthouse in his construction. The tower is sixty-five feet tall with a base diameter of twenty feet and a top diameter of twelve feet. The walls are almost solid brick, with a header course every nine courses, and are uniformly graduated from four feet thick at the bottom to two feet thick at the top. The tower is capped with a five-inch-thick soapstone deck fourteen feet in diameter

A third-order Fresnel lens was installed in 1857; the oil-powered light was visible from a distance of fourteen miles. Federal troops controlled the lighthouse and surrounding property for a short period during the Civil War. The valuable lens and its components had been removed for safekeeping and delivered to the Confederate Collector of Customs in Apalachicola. Eventually the light was relighted on August 1, 1865. Because this original lens was damaged during the war, it was replaced in 1889. At first, the Fresnel lens was powered by oil, then by electricity supplied by a gasoline-powered generator. The Fresnel lens was replaced with a modern optic lens around 1940. In 1949, the light was automated and lighthouse keepers were no longer needed.

The Cape St. George Lighthouse has withstood battering winds and seas for 150 years, and its long tenure of service places it among the most significant structures of its type.

After the lighthouse had deteriorated for many years, Hurricane Opal in 1995 seemed to ring the death knell for the structure. Wind and sea had weakened the foundation; the result was a leaning tower. The Cape St. George Lighthouse Society was established to save the historic structure. After three years of constant effort and dedication, the small group of volunteers slated September 20, 1999, as the completion date of phase one of the restoration. Phase one was the stabilization of the lighthouse in a perpendicular position on a uniquely fortified foundation. However, as of this writing, the lighthouse remains in serious jeopardy.

▭ Site Facts ▬

Date of Construction: 1852
First Lighted: 1852
Tower Height (ground to top of lantern): 74 feet
Focal Plane: 72 feet
Architect: unknown
Builders: Edward Bowden
Type of Construction: conical brick tower
Foundation Materials: brick
Construction Materials: brick and iron
Number of Steps: unknown
Daymark: white conical tower with a black lantern
Active: no

Deactivated: May 19, 1994

Original Lighting Apparatus: fifteen fixed Lewis lamps with sixteen-inch reflectors

Manufacturer and Date: Winslow Lewis (1843)

Other Apparatus Used: third-order fixed Fresnel lens

Manufacturer and Date: Henry-LePaute (1857)

Other Apparatus Used: third-order fixed Fresnel lens

Manufacturer and Date: unknown (1889)

Modern Optics: 300mm lantern (1977)

Present Optic: none

Characteristic: fixed white light (originally); flashing white every ten seconds (1949–1977); flashing white every six seconds (1977–1994)

Auxiliary Historic Structures: keeper's dwelling and oil storage house virtually destroyed by hurricanes

National Register Listing: yes

Operating Entity: uncertain as of this writing; probably will go to local state wildlife refuge as a historic site, perhaps to be operated by the Cape St. George Lighthouse Society

Tower Open to the Public: no   **Lighthouse Museum:** no

Hours: none

Gift Shop: no   **Handicapped Access:** no

Contact: Cape St. George Lighthouse Society, P.O. Box 915, Apalachicola, FL 32329; (850) 653-8869

Directions:

From the Crooked River Lighthouse, continue west on US 98 into Apalachicola. The Cape St. George Lighthouse is at the southern tip of Cape St. George on Little St. George Island and is not visible from Apalachicola. The lighthouse can be reached only by boat. There is a boat ramp in town, and several boat rental and tour companies in Apalachicola can accommodate visitors. Contact Eco Ventures, Inc., P.O. Box 578, Apalachicola, FL 32329, (850) 653-2593, for suggestions.

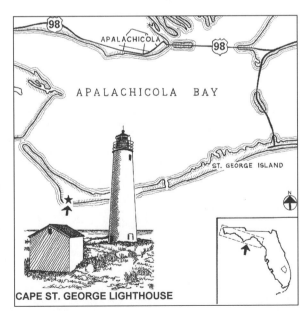

CAPE ST. GEORGE LIGHTHOUSE

ST. GEORGE'S ISLAND LIGHTHOUSE

(Lighthouse Site Only)

LITTLE ST. GEORGE ISLAND, NEAR APALACHICOLA, FLORIDA

By Thomas W. Taylor

I n the late 1820s, the new port of Apalachicola was growing rapidly, handling most of the commerce from several agricultural counties in Georgia, Alabama, and Florida. To help provide for the safe entrance of vessels into St. George's Sound and Apalachicola Bay, the Florida territorial legislature, in 1829, passed a resolution requesting its Congressional delegates to obtain an appropriation for the building of a lighthouse. In 1831, Congress finally authorized the building of a lighthouse on the west end of St. George's Island for $11,400.

At first, there was some delay and confusion, as the Fifth Auditor of the Treasury, the man who was responsible for building and maintaining America's lighthouses had chosen the collector of customs from St. Marks to locate a site for and build the lighthouse. The Fifth Auditor had not known that Apalachicola now had its own collector of customs, who should have been in charge of the lighthouses in his area.

When the people of Apalachicola found out that a man from St. Marks would locate and oversee their lighthouse, they were indignant. The public pressure led the Fifth Auditor to appoint the Apalachicola collector to the task. Unfortunately, all of this delayed the construction of the new lighthouse.

Finally, in May 1833, Winslow Lewis received the contract for "building a lighthouse and dwelling house on the west end of St. George's Island." Both structures were completed that fall. Like many of the lighthouses in this section of Florida, the new lighthouse on St. George's Island was damaged in numerous storms and several major hurricanes. Because of this, this lighthouse was often "in bad order." After a major hurricane in 1842, the lighthouse was repaired and received fifteen new lamps with sixteen-inch reflectors. The local lighthouse superintendent could then report "everything [is] in good repair and condition."

As commercial traffic in the gulf increased, mariners needed a coastal aid to navigation on Cape St. George that would help them steer past the shoals, and the St. George's Island Lighthouse on the west end of the island did not serve this purpose. A movement was started to build a new lighthouse on Cape St. George. Finally, in 1846, after Florida had become a state, Congress acceded to the demand for the new lighthouse. The contractor was permitted to tear down the St. George's Island Lighthouse and use its materials to build the new lighthouse two miles to the southeast. The lighting apparatus from the old tower was transferred to the new lighthouse. This new tower, the first Cape St. George Lighthouse, was a near duplicate of the old St. George's Island Lighthouse and was lighted on March 3, 1848. Today, no major ruins of this lighthouse exist, but some brick rubble has been found on the west end of what today is called Little St. George Island.

▭ Site Facts ▬

Date of Construction: 1833

First Lighted: late 1833

Tower Height (ground to top of lantern): 75 feet

Focal Plane: 70 feet

Architect: Winslow Lewis

Builder: Winslow Lewis

Type of Construction: conical brick tower

Foundation Materials: brick

Construction Materials: brick, soapstone, and iron

Number of Steps: unknown

Daymark: whitewashed brick with black lantern

Active: no

Deactivated: mid-1847

Original Lighting Apparatus: thirteen Lewis patent lamps with sixteen-inch reflectors (1833–1843)

Manufacturer and Date: Winslow Lewis (1833)

Other Apparatus Used: fifteen Lewis patent lamps with sixteen-inch reflectors (1843–1847)

Manufacturer and Date: Winslow Lewis (1843)

Modern Optics: none

Present Optic: none

Characteristic: fixed white light

Auxiliary Historic Structures: none surviving

National Register Listing: yes

Operating Entity: none

Tower Open to the Public: tower is no longer in existence

Lighthouse Museum: no

Hours: none

Gift Shop: no

Handicapped Access: no

Directions:

From the Cape St. George Lighthouse (see previous chapter), you can walk or boat the 2 miles to the western tip of Little St. George Island, where this lighthouse was located. There is an excellent boat ramp in town, and there are several boat rental and tour companies in Apalachicola that can accommodate

ST. GEORGE'S ISLAND LIGHTHOUSE

visitors. Contact EcoVentures, Inc., at P.O. Box 578, Apalachicola, FL 32329, (850) 653-2593 for suggestions.

CAPE SAN BLAS LIGHTHOUSE

NEAR PORT ST. JOE, FLORIDA

By Herman and Trip Jones

Cape San Blas, sometimes referred to as the "Hatteras of the Gulf," juts fourteen miles into the gulf before sixty feet of water is found. Consequently, numerous wrecks lie buried beneath its shifting sands, along with three lighthouses. The cape holds the dubious honor of having the most towers constructed (four) and destroyed (three) of any Florida lighthouse site.

The first brick tower was completed in April 1848. This sixty-five-foot-tall lighthouse was destroyed only three years later during a hurricane in August 1851. A second brick tower was completed and lighted in November 1855. This tower promptly fell during another hurricane only ten months later. A third brick tower was completed and its new third-order lens was lighted on May 1, 1859. During the Civil War, the keeper's houses and all wooden structures were burned by the Confederates in order to deny use by the Union army, but the tower survived. The lens and clockwork apparatus had been removed by the Confederate lighthouse superintendent prior to the attack on the lighthouse. It was relighted on July 15, 1866. At ninety-six feet above sea level, the light could be seen sixteen miles into the gulf as it flashed every ninety seconds.

By 1870, the gulf was washing the base of the tower during gales. Later, the tower stood in eight feet of water, and in calm seas the keepers rowed to the tower to light the lantern. In rough seas, a sixth-order, white, fixed light was hoisted on a pole onshore, which was visible eleven miles out into the gulf. Finally, on July 3, 1882, the "handsome" tower tumbled into the gulf. Its position is now marked on nautical charts as an obstruction in twenty feet of water.

On June 30, 1885, the iron skeletal tower that overlooks the cape today was lighted using the old third-order lens. Its lighting had been delayed by an outbreak of malaria among the workmen, by a severe drought, and by the sinking of the ship that was transporting the materials. Luckily, the ship sank in shallow water near Sanibel Island, and the iron tower was salvaged. This tower was built ninety-eight feet above sea level and fifteen hundred feet from shore. The incessant erosion continued, however, and in only three years that distance was shortened to only two hundred feet. In 1894, a hurricane again placed the tower in the surf and wrecked the dwelling of keeper William M. Quinn.

In April 1896, the light was temporarily discontinued as work progressed towards dismantling the tower and moving it to a new location on Black's Island. Twenty thousand dollars was originally appropriated for this move, but the money was spent after work on only one dwelling and the tower base was completed. The tower was temporarily stabilized on its original site; the lens was brought out of storage and relighted.

In 1900, Congress appropriated $15,000 to move the tower over one mile to the north of the cape, but currents began to rebuild the cape shoreline. As a result, the move was canceled and the light remained in its original location for another sixteen years. The 1915 and 1916 hurricanes eroded the beaches once again, and the tower eventually stood six hundred feet from shore. Finally, in 1918, it was moved 1,857 feet to its present location.

On January 18, 1996, the light was discontinued by the Coast Guard, and its exquisite 1906 Barbier, Bénard et Turenne bivalve lens was covered. Hurricane Earl, in September 1998, undermined one of the two turn-of-the-century keeper's houses and left it sitting precariously on the beach and vulnerable to the surf. After nine months of being buffeted by storm waves, the house was finally moved, along with its sister cottage, to the base of the lighthouse, where they are currently in the process of being restored. A museum and gift shop are planned.

▭ Site **Facts** ▬

Date of Construction: 1885
First Lighted: June 30, 1885
Tower Height (ground to top of lantern): 96 feet
Focal Plane: 101 feet
Architect: unknown
Builders: Phoenix Ironworks, Ocean City, NJ
Type of Construction: iron skeletal tower
Foundation Materials: concrete
Construction Materials: iron pilings
Number of Steps (ground to lantern room): 138 (approximately)
Daymark: white square pyramidal skeletal tower enclosing stair column and black lantern
Active: no
Deactivated: January 18, 1996
Original Lighting Apparatus: 1859 third-order revolving Fresnel lens from old tower
Manufacturer and Date: unknown
Other Apparatus Used: third-order bivalve lens
Manufacturer and Date: Barbier, Bénard et Turenne (1906)
Modern Optics: none
Present Optic: 1906 third-order bivalve lens, complete with original clockworks and weight
Characteristic: white flash every twenty seconds (originally); none (currently)
Auxiliary Historic Structures: two keepers' dwellings, brick oil storage house
National Register Listing: no
Operating Entity: Eglin Air Force Base
Tower Open to the Public: no
Lighthouse Museum: no
Hours: none
Gift Shop: no
Handicapped Access: no
Contact: Director of Environmental Management, 501 DeLeon Street, Bldg. 696, Suite 101, Eglin Air Force Base, FL 32542-5133; (850) 882-4437; e-mail: newberry@ntserver.eglin.af.mil

Directions:

From Apalachicola, take US 98 west, then State Route 30 to State Route 30E (Cape San Blas Road). Follow Route 30E 2.4 miles to U.S. Air Force Radar Station, then .4 miles to the Lighthouse Road on the left, marked U.S. Air Force, Cape San Blas. The lighthouse sits .5 miles down this road on the right amongst the tall, longleaf pines. The property is now closed, but it can be viewed from the road or from the beach, which is open to the public. If the Air Force Road is closed, it is often possible to travel 1.2 miles further along Route 30E to the Stumphole Beach Access. Park and walk 1 mile south on the public beach.

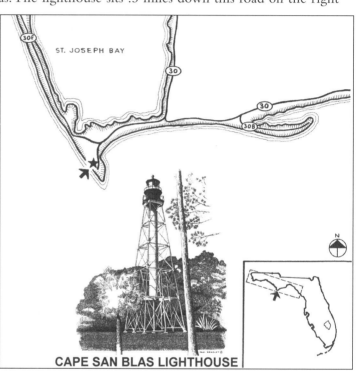

CAPE SAN BLAS LIGHTHOUSE

ST. JOSEPH'S BAY
LIGHTHOUSE
(Lighthouse Site Only)

NEAR PORT ST. JOE, FLORIDA

By Thomas W. Taylor

I n the 1830s, an important new boomtown sprang up on Florida's gulf coast. Located on the east shore of St. Joseph's Bay, the city of St. Joseph would later become a terminus of Florida's first railroad and site of the convention that drew up the first state constitution for the proposed state of Florida.

Because of the increasing commerce to this new port, the Legislative Council of the Territory of Florida passed a resolution in 1836 asking that a lighthouse be erected on one of the points at the entrance to St. Joseph's Bay. On March 3, 1837, Congress appropriated $10,000 for the construction of the lighthouse. It took more than a year to select the site and secure the title to the land, but finally, in the fall of 1838, the new lighthouse was under construction. It was completed on February 23, 1839, and the fourteen lamps of its light were lighted shortly thereafter.

For a couple of years, the St. Joseph's Bay Lighthouse was the best kept and most efficient of the lighthouses in the Apalachicola District. The lighthouse even weathered storms without any problem. However, in 1841, a ship carrying yellow fever entered the port of St. Joseph, and the town's population was soon decimated by an epidemic. Between the plague and the storms, the town's economy was destroyed. Before long, the few remaining citizens of St. Joseph had had enough, and the town was completely abandoned. Commerce now bypassed the area to which it had formerly been attracted.

However, commerce to the town of Apalachicola to the east was increasing, and more and more, large oceanic vessels were coasting the shores of Florida on their way to the growing port. The commercial interests of Apalachicola realized that the larger, coastal, commercial vessels needed a major landfall light at Cape San Blas rather than at St. Joseph's Bay.

In 1842, the Apalachicola Chamber of Commerce declared in a Memorial to Congress that "In erecting a Light House at St. Joseph's Bay, the location has proved . . . unfortunate, being . . . a harbor light and in no degree useful to Commerce, as that port is entirely abandoned for commercial purposes." Ship captains also joined the fray to change the lighthouse to Cape San Blas.

In 1843, the Collector of Customs at Apalachicola declared that the St. Joseph's Bay Lighthouse was in poor condition, and the decision was made to abandon the lighthouse. In 1846, contracts were let to build the new Cape San Blas Lighthouse to the south, and the contractors were given "the right to use the materials of the old lighthouse . . . as far as they could." The old tower was torn down, and the bricks, lantern, and lighting apparatus were moved south to Cape San Blas. Today, little is left of the St. Joseph's Bay Lighthouse. A few years ago, the Florida Park Service unknowingly bulldozed through what was left of the lighthouse's foundation. Only a few scattered bricks and pieces remain on the shore today.

▭ Site Facts ▬

Date of Construction: 1839
First Lighted: March 1839
Tower Height (ground to top of lantern): 55 feet
Focal Plane: 50 feet
Architect: unknown
Builders: unknown
Type of Construction: conical brick tower
Foundation Materials: brick
Construction Materials: brick, soapstone, and iron
Number of Steps (ground to lantern room): unknown
Daymark: whitewashed brick conical tower with black lantern
Active: no

Deactivated: fall 1846

Original Lighting Apparatus: fourteen Lewis patent lamps with sixteen-inch reflectors (1839–1846)

Manufacturer and Date: Winslow Lewis (1839)

Other Apparatus Used: none

Manufacturer and Date: none

Modern Optics: none

Present Optic: none

Auxiliary Historic Structures: none surviving

Tower Open to the Public: no

Lighthouse Museum: no

Hours: none

Gift Shop: no

Handicapped Access: no

Directions:

From the Cape San Blas Lighthouse, retrace your route to State Route 30E. Turn left (west) onto Route 30E and continue to follow it into the St. Joseph Peninsula State Park. The light-house site is on the east shore of the peninsula some distance from the last parking area. Whether any of the park rangers can direct you to the exact site is doubtful.

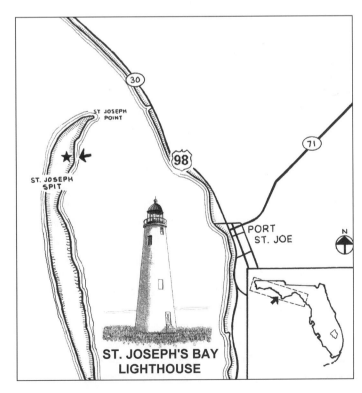

ST. JOSEPH'S BAY
LIGHTHOUSE

ST. JOSEPH POINT LIGHTHOUSE

NEAR PORT ST. JOE, FLORIDA

By Danny Raffield

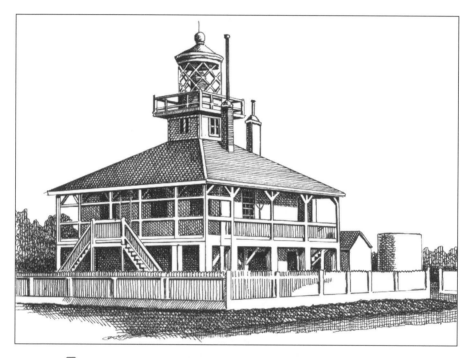

Although early Spanish and French explorers established a presence on the shores of St. Joseph's Bay, they did not stay, and the bay's sparsely populated shore stayed mostly unchanged until 1836, when the town of St. Joseph was founded. The town was a miracle of expansion, and with the increased commerce, a lighthouse was needed at the entrance to the bay. On January 4, 1839, the government took possession of the new St. Joseph's Bay Lighthouse, which was located a short distance inside the peninsula marking the harbor's entrance. After the economy of the town collapsed due to a yellow fever epidemic, the lighthouse was decommissioned in late 1846.

The bay was without a lighthouse until 1901. At this time, Congress agreed to fund a new light. Engineers were sent to survey the old site inside the St. Joseph Peninsula. After reconsidering, a new site was found a few miles to the north, across the bay on the mainland. President William McKinley signed a work order, and the

St. Joseph Point Lighthouse was opened in 1902. Its function was to mark the harbor up to 13 miles offshore plus serve as a rear range light with a smaller light placed 660 feet in front of it. The smaller lantern of the front range light had to be raised each evening by block and tackle; it could be seen up to six miles offshore. By aligning the two lights, a vessel could travel the deepest water into the harbor.

As St. Joseph's Bay is the only deep-water harbor between Tampa and Pensacola, during World War II, most Allied ships navigating this section of Florida's coast tried to anchor in this harbor at night for safety from enemy submarines. It was common to see numerous ships at anchor here before sunset. At the lighthouse, the ground-level section was enclosed to make living quarters for the Coast Guardsmen. Their job was to patrol the beaches on horseback and guard against German spies, who were known to use moonless nights to sneak ashore from the submarines that prowled the Gulf of Mexico in search of ships to sink. One evening, the sighting of a surfacing submarine silhouetted against the setting sun was reported to the senior officer at the lighthouse. A few days later, on June 29, 1942, a 465-foot British cargo vessel, the *Empire Mica*, was torpedoed and sunk off the shore of Cape San Blas. It is believed that the captain of the submarine was using the St. Joseph Point Lighthouse and range to navigate the deeper waters of the channel into the harbor.

The light served until 1955, when it was replaced by an automated light atop a seventy-five-foot metal tower. Five years later, the lighthouse was declared surplus and was sold at auction for $300. The Coast Guard had removed the lantern, leaving only the lantern gallery. Due to the height of the house, the lantern gallery and watchroom had to be removed in preparation for the lighthouse's first move, six miles to the north. During this process, the lantern gallery was dropped, reducing it to scrap. Afterwards, there was no effort toward restoration.

The lighthouse sat at ground level as a two-story dwelling for its first owner. A few years later, under its second owner, the house served as a hay barn for the numerous cows that were fed from its porches. In 1970, a third owner purchased the house and started a restoration project involving a twenty-three-mile move south to the edge of St. Joseph's Bay. The restoration is now near completion.

▭ Site Facts ▬

Dates of Construction: 1901–1902
First Lighted: August 1, 1902
Tower Height (ground to top of lantern): 41 feet
Focal Plane: 63 feet
Architect: unknown
Builders: unknown
Type of Construction: frame house-style tower
Foundation Materials: brick

Construction Materials: wood

Number of Steps: (ground to lantern room) 40

Daymark: white tower with black lantern on square, white, red-roofed dwelling on brick piers

Active: no   **Deactivated:** 1955

Original Lighting Apparatus: third-order fixed Fresnel lens

Manufacturer and Date: Barbier, Bénard et Turenne (1901)

Other Apparatus Used: none

Manufacturer and Date: none

Modern Optics: none

Present Optic: none

Characteristic: fixed white light (originally); changed by an electrical flasher unit to four-second white flash followed by six-second eclipse (1936–1955); flashing white every six seconds (new tower)

Auxiliary Historic Structures: none

National Register Listing: no

Operating Entity: private residence

Tower Open to the Public: no   **Lighthouse Museum:** no

Hours: none

Gift Shop: no   **Handicapped Access:** no

Directions:

From the site of the St. Joseph's Bay Lighthouse, retrace your route back down State Route 30E past the road leading to the Cape San Blas Lighthouse to the intersection with State Route 30. Turn left (north) and follow this road about 3 miles. The lighthouse is located at 2071 State Road 30, 3 miles south of the intersection with Highway US 98 (south of Port St. Joe). No tours of the lighthouse are available, but the owners, the Raffields, do not mind people taking exterior pictures of it for nonprofit purposes. There is parking along the roadside.

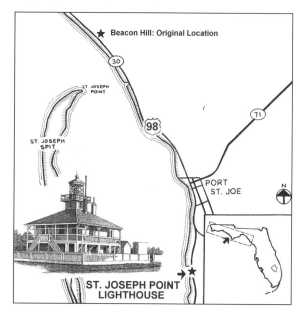

PENSACOLA LIGHTHOUSE (1824)

(Lighthouse Site Only)

PENSACOLA, FLORIDA

By Thomas W. Taylor

I n the 1820s, Pensacola became the most important harbor of the Territory of Florida on the gulf coast. The city had already had a long and distinguished history as a major Spanish settlement and as the capital of British West Florida, a designation the Spanish retained when they returned in 1784. It was here that Gen. Andrew Jackson, the first U.S. governor of Florida, received the transfer of the province from Spain.

To better direct the vastly expanding gulf coastal trade into the excellent harbor and port of Pensacola, the Florida Territorial Legislature sent a Memorial to President James Monroe in September 1822, declaring the "necessity of erecting" a lighthouse at Pensacola. On March 3, 1823, Congress passed an act appropriating $6,000 to build the lighthouse. While the lighthouse was under construction, the lightship *Aurora Borealis* was assigned to the Pensacola station. She was the second lightship ever used in the United States.

In April 1824, Winslow Lewis was awarded the contract to build the thirty-foot brick tower, erect the seven-foot lantern, outfit the tower with his patent Argand lamps, and build the one-story, two-room, brick keeper's dwelling. Lewis would do the work for $5,735. Originally, the lighthouse was to be outfitted with a fixed light, but for $400 more, Lewis included a revolving light. Work was begun in October 1824 and completed in mid-December. The lighthouse was first lighted on December 20, 1824, and was the first lighthouse completed on Florida's gulf coast. The *Pensacola Gazette* announced: "The new Light-House at the entrance of our harbor . . . equals our most sanguine expectations."

But all did not work perfectly. Keeper Jeremiah Ingraham found that the lamp's rotation mechanism was so poorly made that it continually failed. It was finally taken to the naval base, where it was completely rebuilt with successful results. Other problems appeared. The whitewash on the bricks began to wash off. The mortar between the bricks was too soft; it began to dissolve in the rain and water penetrated the walls of the tower. The tower was coated with Roman cement to waterproof it. Additionally, the glass of the lantern was of such poor quality that it began to become cloudy and discolored in the intense Florida sunlight. The glass finally became opaque, obscuring the light, and mariners complained of its dim quality. Other mariners complained that the light was blocked by trees. Finally, in 1847, new glass was installed in the lighthouse; other major repairs finally made it a first-class light.

However, a new problem arose. In the years since the lighthouse was built, the entrance channel into Pensacola Bay had begun to shift westward, and by the 1850s the lighthouse was no longer effective for navigation in its original location. The new Lighthouse Board decided to build an entirely new lighthouse about one half mile to the west on another bluff. This new 150-foot lighthouse, which still stands today, was completed and first lighted on January 1, 1859. The old tower was discontinued and abandoned. It was eventually torn down, but it is not absolutely known when this occurred. There are references to it during the Civil War, but within a few years after that, it was gone. The Fort Barrancas Range Lights would eventually be built on or near the site of the first Pensacola Lighthouse.

▭ Site **Facts** ▬▬

Date of Construction: 1824
First Lighted: December 20, 1824
Tower Height: thirty feet plus seven-foot lantern
Focal Plane: 80 feet
Architect: Winslow Lewis
Builder: Benjamin Beall
Type of Construction: conical brick tower

Foundation Materials: brick
Construction Materials: brick and iron
Number of Steps: unknown
Daymark: white conical tower with black lantern
Active: no
Deactivated: 1859
Original Lighting Apparatus: ten revolving patent lamps with fourteen-inch reflectors
Manufacturer and Date: Winslow Lewis (1824)
Other Apparatus Used: ten revolving patent lamps with sixteen-inch reflectors
Manufacturer and Date: Winslow Lewis (1847)
Modern Optics: none
Present Optics: none
Characteristic: white flash every thirty-five seconds
Auxiliary Historic Structures: none surviving
National Register Listing: no
Operating Entity: United States Navy
Tower Open to the Public: no
Lighthouse Museum: no
Hours: none
Gift Shop: no
Handicapped Access: none

Directions:

After leaving the St. Joseph Point Lighthouse, continue on State Route 30, then follow US 98 west through Port St. Joe. About 8 miles north of Port St. Joe is the original site of the St. Joseph Point Lighthouse. Today, near Beacon Hill, this site is marked by the still-active, steel, skeletal tower that replaced the lighthouse in 1960. From there, continue on US 98 through Panama City to Pensacola. When coming into Pensacola, continue straight to US 29. Turn left (south) onto Old Palafox Highway. Bear right (west) on State Route 292 (Pace Boulevard), which becomes Barrancas Avenue, and go 3 miles. Turn left (south) onto State Route 295 (Army Road), which leads to the main gate of the Pensacola Naval Air Station. Get cleared through the main gate and continue straight to Mustin Beach Road. Turn right (west) and follow this road until you see Fort Barrancas on your right. The site of the first Pensacola Lighthouse is about midway between Fort Barrancas and the present Pensacola Lighthouse to the west. The next left will take you to the Navy Lodge, which stands on the bluff just west of where the dwelling and tower once stood. A recent archeological excavation located the brick piers for the dwelling and a number of artifacts. Unfortunately, this site is slated to become part of a larger parking area for the Navy Lodge, and some rubble that may have come from the lighthouse has been tossed down the bluff.

FIRST PENSACOLA LIGHTHOUSE

FORT BARRANCAS
REAR RANGE LIGHT
(Lighthouse Site Only)
PENSACOLA, FLORIDA

By Neil Hurley

To better mark the entrance channel into Pensacola Bay, the Fort Barrancas range lights were constructed in 1859 "as ranges for crossing the bar and making a safe anchorage at night." It is not clear if there was a dwelling associated with these early lights.

The lights were extinguished only two years later at the start of the Civil War. In 1867, the lights were relighted, after a delay "being caused by the failure of the keeper to report for duty." Again, the lights did not last for very long, for only eleven months later they were discontinued, since it was felt they were no longer necessary for commerce in Pensacola.

The Fort Barrancas Range Lights were reestablished in 1888 near the site of the first Pensacola Lighthouse. The rear light was located on a wooden frame tower, with a small two-room house for the keeper nearby. The dwelling was increased in size when two rooms, a kitchen and dining room, were added in 1897.

Few details of the life of the keepers at this station are known. Keeper William J. Doyle was one of twenty gulf coast lighthouse keepers commended for "performing their duties under hazardous and unusual conditions" during the hurricane of 1917. Their duties consisted mainly of maintaining the lights at full intensity under trying circumstances, recovering property that had been washed away, giving refuge to people in the area, and making temporary repairs after the storm.

The Fort Barrancas Range Lights were unmanned before 1920 and discontinued in 1930. Today nothing remains of this light station.

Site Facts

Dates of Construction: 1859, 1888
First Lighted: 1859
Tower Height: unknown
Focal Plane: 54 feet
Architect: unknown
Builders: unknown
Type of Construction: wood skeletal tower
Foundation Materials: brick piles
Construction Materials: wood
Number of Steps: none (a ladder was used)
Daymark: red (later changed to white), square, pyramidal structure covered with horizontal slats on four piles
Active: no
Deactivated: 1930
Original Lighting Apparatus: small lens lantern
Manufacturer and Date: unknown
Other Apparatus Used: steamer lantern
Present Optics: none
Characteristic: fixed white light
Auxiliary Historic Structures: none surviving
Tower Open to the Public: no (grounds are in a public area)
National Register Listing: no
Operating Entity: United States Navy
Lighthouse Museum: no
Hours: none
Gift Shop: no
Handicapped Access: none

Directions:

The location for this range light is on or near the site of the first Pensacola Lighthouse (see Pensacola Lighthouse section). The Navy Lodge, a hotel for service members, now stands on the bluff where the dwelling and tower of the Fort Barrancas Rear Range Light once stood.

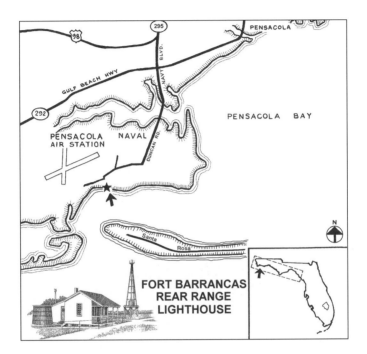

PENSACOLA
LIGHTHOUSE (1859)

PENSACOLA, FLORIDA

By Thomas M. Garner

Although the harbor at Pensacola had been known by French and Spanish explorers as one of the finest on the gulf coast, it was the United States that first erected a lighthouse here in 1824. That first lighthouse was soon deemed ineffective because of the primitive lighting devices used and because the channel had shifted to the west. In 1852, the new Lighthouse Board began a concerted campaign to modernize and improve the lighthouses of the United States, and a new, tall tower was planned for Pensacola.

In August 1854, Congress appropriated $25,000 to build the new lighthouse and fit it with a new first-order Fresnel lens. However, the sum was not enough, and two years later, an additional $30,000 was appropriated to complete the project. The new 150-foot-tall lighthouse was built on a 50-foot bluff approximately one half mile west of the original Pensacola Lighthouse. Construction began in 1856 and was completed in late 1858. The lamp in the first-order lens was first lighted on January 1, 1859.

Two days after Florida seceded from the Union on January 10, 1861, troops from Florida and Alabama confiscated all Federal property on the mainland, including the lighthouse. Union troops withdrew to the forts on the islands. The Pensacola Lighthouse was the first on the gulf coast to be extinguished by Confederate order, and in May the new Confederate-appointed keeper removed the lighting apparatus from the tower for safekeeping. During 1861, Federal forces on the islands bombarded the Confederate works on the mainland, including the targets of the "Light House Batteries." A number of Union cannon shot hit and bounced off the lighthouse during these bombardments. By May 1862, the Confederates had withdrawn from Pensacola, and on December 20, 1862, the Pensacola Lighthouse was lighted once again with a temporary fourth-order lens.

After the war, the original first-order lens was discovered in the Navy yard, but it soon disappeared, possibly having been sent to New York by the Navy for repair. However, a new first-order lens was ordered, installed, and lighted on April 1, 1869, and this lens remains in the tower today. Also in 1869, a new keeper's dwelling was built. In the 1870s, the white tower was given a more distinctive daymark: the lower third was repainted white and the upper two-thirds were painted black to stand out better against the blue sky.

In the late 1870s, severe cracking was noted in the tower. Considered a result of the Civil War bombardment and severe lightning strikes during the 1870s, the cracks were repaired during a major renovation, which was completed in 1879. Repairs were also made to the lantern, and new glass was installed. The tower received a fresh coat of paint, and the keeper's dwelling was repaired and painted.

After a series of less-than-perfect keepers who served relatively short terms, George T. Clifford became keeper in 1886 and served until his retirement in 1917. During this period, the Pensacola Lighthouse enjoyed a period of relative calm and excellent maintenance.

In 1938, the lighthouse was electrified, and the keeper's dwelling was fitted with all the modern conveniences. A year later, the lighthouse was taken over, as were all lighthouses, by the Coast Guard. The Pensacola Lighthouse was automated in 1965, and plans were developed to demolish the dwelling. However, preservationists won out, and the quarters were leased to the Navy, which still maintains them.

Today, the Pensacola Lighthouse remains an active aid to navigation in the hands of the Coast Guard. A civilian support group, however, has been formed; it hopes to open the tower to visitors on a daily basis.

▭ Site Facts ▬

Dates of Construction: 1856–1858

First Lighted: January 1, 1859

Tower Height: 150 feet

Focal Plane: 191 feet (highest focal plane in Florida)

Architect: unknown

Builder: Capt. John Newton, U.S. Army

Type of Construction: conical brick tower

Foundation Materials: brick

Construction Materials: brick, granite, and iron

Number of Steps: 177

Daymark: conical tower with lower third painted white and upper two-thirds painted black with a black lantern

Active: yes

Deactivated: no

Original Lighting Apparatus: first-order revolving Fresnel lens

Manufacturer and Date: Henry-LePaute (1858)

Other Apparatus Used: fourth-order Fresnel lens

Manufacturer and Date: unknown (installed 1862)

Other Apparatus Used: first-order revolving Fresnel lens

Manufacturer and Date: Henry-LePaute (1868)

Modern Optics: none

Present Optics: first-order revolving Fresnel lens

Manufacturer and Date: Henry-Lepaute (1868)

Characteristic: white flash every twenty seconds

Auxiliary Historic Structures: brick, two-story keeper's dwelling

National Register Listing: yes

Operating Entity: United States Coast Guard

Tower Open to the Public: during weekends from May to October and on special occasions

Lighthouse Museum: yes

Hours: variable

Gift Shop: no

Handicapped Access: no

Contact: Coast Guard Station, Tow Way Street, NAS Pensacola, Pensacola, FL 32508; (850) 455-2354

Directions:

Upon leaving the site of the first Pensacola Lighthouse and the Fort Barrancas Range Light, turn right at the exit from the parking lot, then immediately left onto a dirt road. About .5 miles down this dirt road, you will find the Pensacola Lighthouse and keeper's dwelling to your right. You can park almost anywhere in this area for a stroll around the grounds. Several historical markers of interest are also on the grounds.

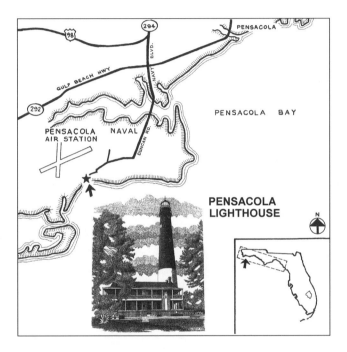

FORT MCREE
REAR RANGE LIGHTS
(Lighthouse Site Only)
PENSACOLA, FLORIDA

By Neil Hurley

Three forts guarded the entrance to Pensacola Bay shortly before the Civil War: Fort McRee, on the west side, was a wing-shaped, brick fort started in 1834; Fort Barrancas was further north on the mainland; and Fort Pickens was located on Santa Rosa Island on the east side of the channel entrance.

A set of range lights was built in 1859 just south of Fort McRee to help guide ships through the deepest part of the channel into the harbor. Although it is not clear if a full-time keeper maintained the lights, an 1861 drawing of Fort McRee shows two small houses almost in range at the location of the lights.

When the Civil War started, Union troops abandoned Forts McRee and Barrancas and fled to Fort Pickens, which they held throughout the war. In November 1861, Union forces opened up a furious bombardment on Confederate positions that turned Fort McRee into a pile of rubble. The range lights did not survive the war, probably having been destroyed by Confederates to prevent their use by Union ships.

The lights were reestablished after the war in 1866 but shone only for a short time before they were destroyed by a hurricane. It was not until 1888 that the range lights were reestablished, with a single keeper in a small house near the rear range tower maintaining the lights. One of the wooden towers marked both Fort McRee Range and Caucus Cut Range. Hurricanes in 1916 and 1917 caused minor damage to the lights, and in 1918 the station was converted to automatic operation.

The ruins of Fort McRee were visible until the 1930s, when the last bit of the old fort was washed into the channel. Nothing is known to remain of the towers or keeper's dwelling today.

Site Facts

Dates of Construction: 1859, 1888
First Lighted: 1859
Tower Height: unknown
Focal Plane: 56 feet
Architect: unknown
Builders: unknown
Type of Construction: wood
Foundation Materials: brick piles
Construction Materials: wood
Number of Steps: none (a ladder was used)
Daymark: red, square, pyramidal structure covered with horizontal slats on four piles
Active: no
Deactivated: 1930
Original Lighting Apparatus: small lens lantern
Manufacturer and Date: unknown
Other Apparatus Used: steamer lantern
Present Optics: none
Characteristic: fixed white light
Auxiliary Historic Structures: none surviving
National Register Listing: no
Operating Entity: part of Gulf Islands National Seashore
Tower Open to the Public: no
Lighthouse Museum: no
Hours: none
Gift Shop: no
Handicapped Access: none

Directions:

The site of this lighthouse is off the eastern end of Perdido Key, which is now part of Gulf Islands National Seashore. The area is accessible by boat or by a long hike to the eastern point of Perdido Key. To go by land, return to Pensacola and take State Route 292 west to Gulf Beach. There, turn left (east) towards Johnson Beach. From the end of the road, it is about a 6-mile hike to the east end of Perdido Key and the site of the Fort McRee Rear Range Light. This is the western terminus of the Florida Lighthouse Trail.

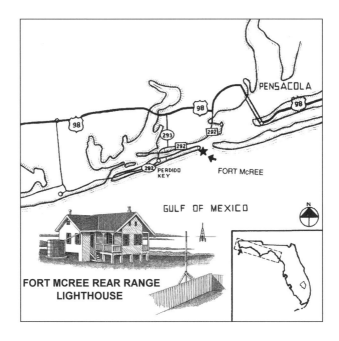

BIBLIOGRAPHY

Bansemer, Roger. *Bansemer's Book of Florida Lighthouses.* Sarasota, Florida: Pineapple Press, Inc., 1999.

Blank, Joan Gill. *Key Biscayne: A History of Miami's Tropical Island and the Cape Florida Lighthouse.* Sarasota, Florida: Pineapple Press, Inc., 1996.

Butler, David F. *Hillsboro Lighthouse.* Pompano Beach, Florida: Pompano Beach Historical Society, 1998.

Childers, Frank M. *History of the Cape Canaveral Lighthouse.* Melbourne, Florida: The Brevard Museum, Inc., 1995.

Cipra, David L. *Lighthouses, Lightships, and the Gulf of Mexico.* Alexandria, Virginia: Cypress Communications, 1997.

Dean, Love. *Reef Lights: Sea-Swept Lighthouses of the Florida Keys.* Key West, Florida: The Historic Key West Preservation Board, 1982.

———. *Lighthouses of the Florida Keys.* Sarasota, Florida: Pineapple Press, Inc., 1998.

De Wire, Elinor. *Guide to Florida Lighthouses.* Sarasota, Florida: Pineapple Press, Inc., 1987. Second edition, 2001.

DuBois, Bessie Wilson. *The History of the Jupiter Lighthouse.* Jupiter, Florida: Bessie Wilson DuBois, 1981.

Garner, Thomas M. *The Pensacola Lighthouse.* Pensacola, Florida: The Pensacola Historical Society, 1994.

Holland, Francis Ross, Jr. *America's Lighthouses: An Illustrated History.* New York: Dover Publications, 1988.

Hurley, Neil. *An Illustrated History of Cape Florida Lighthouse.* Camino, California: Historic Lighthouse Publishers, 1989.

———. *Keepers of Florida Lighthouses, 1821–1939.* Alexandria, Virginia: Historic Lighthouse Publishers, 1990.

———. *Lighthouses of the Dry Tortugas: An Illustrated History.* Aies, Hawaii: Historic Lighthouse Publishers, 1994.

LeBuff, Charles. *Sanybel Light: A Historical Autobiography.* Sanibel, Florida: Amber Publishing, 1998.

McCarthy, Kevin M., and William L. Trotter. *Florida Lighthouses.* Gainesville, Florida: University of Florida Press, 1990.

Spinella, Teri. "St. Augustine Lighthouse." *The Keeper's Log*, vol. 2 (winter 1989): 3–7.

———. *History of the St. Augustine Lighthouse.* Lake Buena Vista, Florida: Artworks, 1992.

Taylor, Thomas W. *The Beacon of Mosquito Inlet: A History of the Ponce de Leon Inlet Lighthouse.* Allandale, Florida: Thomas W. Taylor, 1993.

———. "Building the Ponce de Leon Inlet Lighthouse." *The Keeper's Log*, XI:1 (fall 1994): 2–9.

———. "The First Key West Lighthouse." *The Keeper's Log*, XI:3 (spring 1995): 16–22.

———. "The Second Key West Lighthouse." *The Keeper's Log,* XI:4 (summer 1995): 2–15.

———. *Florida's Territorial Lighthouses, 1821–1845: A Legacy of Concern for the Mariner.* Allandale, Florida: Thomas W. Taylor, 1995.

Woodman, Jim. *Key Biscayne: The Romance of Cape Florida.* Key Biscayne, Florida: Jim Woodman, 1972.

GLOSSARY

Active: a lighthouse or aid to navigation that is still in operation

Aid to Navigation: a natural landmark or man-made structure or object, such as a lighthouse, that serves to help mariners navigate

Beacon: a lighted or unlighted aid to navigation (Unlighted beacons are called day-beacons.)

Catodioptric Apparatus: an illuminating device, such as a Fresnel lens, that both reflects catoptic) and refracts (dioptric) light.

Catoptic Apparatus: an illuminating device that reflects light, such as the Lewis patent lamp

Characteristic: the audible, visual, or electronic signal displayed by an aid to navigation

Conical Tower: a lighthouse tower built with a wide base that tapers to a narrow top, like a cone

Daybeacon: a beacon or aid to navigation that does not include a light

Dayboard: the daytime identifier of a channel marker or minor aid to navigation in one of several standard shapes (square, triangle, or rectangle) and colors (red, green, white, orange, yellow, or black)

Daymark: the daytime identifier of an aid to navigation, such as the special identify-ing paint scheme of a lighthouse

Deactivate (Decommission, Discontinue): To remove an aid to navigation from operation

Dwelling: the structure that serves as a home for a lighthouse keeper

Eclipse: the period of darkness in the flashing characteristic of a signal

Establish: to place an authorized aid to navigation in operation for the first time

Fifth-Order: a small Fresnel lens measuring about one foot ten inches tall and just a little over a foot in diameter

First-Order: the largest standard-sized Fresnel lens measuring about eight and a half feet tall and over six feet in diameter

Fixed Light: a light characteristic that is steady

Fixed and Flashing Light: a light characteristic in which a fixed light is combined with a flashing light of higher luminous intensity

Flashing Light: a light characteristic that flashes, created either by a revolving lens with bull's-eye or "flash" lens panels or by an electric flasher unit; the total duration of light in a period is shorter than the total duration of darkness

Focal Plane: the height of an aid to navigation's light above sea level

Fourth-Order: a small Fresnel lens measuring about two and a half feet tall and one and a half feet in diameter

Fresnel, Augustin Jean: French physicist who developed the Fresnel lens

Fresnel Lens: the lens developed by Augustin Jean Fresnel, which consists of a series of prisms arranged so that they magnify and focus light

Groins: rock jetties built to prevent the erosion of coastal sand

Group Flashing: a light characteristic in which a specific number of flashes is regularly repeated

Illuminating Apparatus: a device used to create light in a lighthouse, especially one that uses lenses (same as lighting apparatus or optic)

Keeper: the person who tends the light in a lighthouse

Lantern: the section of the lighthouse tower that protects the lighting apparatus and sometimes includes a watchroom

Lantern Room: the section or room of the lantern where the illuminating apparatus or light is located

Lens: a structure consisting of prisms that magnify and focus light in a lighthouse

Lewis Patent Lamp: the oil lamp with parabolic reflectors developed by Winslow Lewis about 1810 for use in American lighthouses

Light: a term commonly used to refer to the illuminating apparatus or optic of a lighthouse or the signal emitted by a lighted aid to navigation; sometimes misused to refer to the lighthouse itself

Light List: an annual publication of the U.S. Coast Guard and Department of Transportation that lists all aids to navigation as a guide to mariners

Lighthouse: a lighted beacon of major importance that has a full-time resident keeper

Lighting Apparatus: a device used to create light in a lighthouse (same as illuminating apparatus or optic)

Light Station: the compound enclosing and including the lighthouse, keeper's dwellings, oil storage house, and all other outbuildings and structures pertinent to the maintenance of the aid to navigation

Luminous Range: the greatest distance a light is expected to be seen

Modern Optic: a modern, easily replaceable lantern and lens combination

Nautical Miles: the measurement system generally used to describe distances at sea; one nautical mile equals two thousand yards

Occulting: a light characteristic in which the duration of light is longer than the duration of darkness and the intervals of darkness (eclipses) are usually of equal duration

Operating Entity: the owner, operator, or manager of a lighthouse or light station

Optic: a device used to create light in a lighthouse, especially one that uses lenses (same as illuminating apparatus or lighting apparatus)

Pile: a long, heavy timber, iron girder, or concrete post driven into a seabed or riverbed to serve as a support for a lighthouse or other aid to navigation

Present Optic: the illuminating apparatus currently being used in a lighthouse to provide its navigational light

Primary Light: a major light or aid to navigation that once would have required a resident keeper

Private Aid to Navigation: an aid to navigation that is maintained by an individual, organization, or government body other than the U.S. Coast Guard

RACON: radar beacons that, when triggered by pulses from a vessel's radar, will transmit a coded reply to the vessel's radar to identify the RACON station

Radio Beacon: an early electronic navigation system by which a mariner, using a radio direction finder, can locate his position relative to the radio beacon

Range: a channel marked by lights that can be lined up to help the mariner navigate the channel

Range Lights: lights that form a range to help mariners navigate a channel; in general, a front range light is lower and nearer to the mariner than a rear range light

Red Sector: an area, or arc, of the signal of a lighthouse that shows a red light to indicate a danger area; created by placing a red-colored glass or lens in front of the necessary area of the optic of the lighthouse

Screwpile: a specially designed pile that can be screwed into the bottom of the seabed, particularly into coral and rock, for the support of a lighthouse or other aids to navigation

Seacoast Lights: lighthouses constructed for the oceanic navigation of a nation's coastline

Second-Order: a large Fresnel lens measuring nearly seven feet tall and more than four and a half feet in diameter

Secondary Light: a lesser, or minor, aid to navigation where no resident keeper is required

Sixth-Order: the smallest size of Fresnel lens measuring one and a half feet tall and one foot in diameter

Skeletal (or Skeleton) Tower: a tower, usually of iron or steel, constructed of heavy corner members and various horizontal and diagonal bracing members to support the lantern of a lighthouse or other aid to navigation

Third-Order: a medium-sized Fresnel lens measuring a little more than five feet tall and more than three feet in diameter

Tower: the brick, masonry, or iron structure that supports the lantern of a lighthouse

Tower Height: the height of a lighthouse from the ground to the top of the lantern

Watchroom: the area directly below the lantern room in which the keepers stand watch and from which they can monitor the quality of their light

VISITING STATUS FOR FLORIDA LIGHTHOUSES

LIGHTHOUSES OPEN TO THE PUBLIC

1) **St. Augustine Lighthouse, St. Augustine.** Built 1871; restored 1994–95. Original first-order Fresnel lens. Open daily 9:30 A.M. to 5:30 P.M. Later summer hours start in late May. Admission is $5.00 for adults, $3.00 for seniors, and $2.00 for children. Children must be 7 years old and at least 4 feet tall to climb the tower. Includes restored keeper's dwelling, museum, and gift shop. Contact:

> Lighthouse Museum of St. Augustine
> 81 Lighthouse Avenue
> St. Augustine, FL 32084
> (904) 829-0745
> e-mail: stauglh@aug.com
> website: http://www.stauglight.com

2) **Ponce de Leon Inlet Lighthouse, south of Daytona Beach.** Built 1887. Only Florida lighthouse listed as a national historic landmark; second tallest in the U.S. Open daily 10:00 A.M. to 5:00 P.M. (last museum/lighthouse admission at 4:00 P.M.); May 1st through Labor Day 10:00 A.M. to 9:00 P.M. (last admission at 8:00 P.M.). Admission is $4.00 for adults and $1.00 for children 11 and under. Includes three keeper's dwellings as museums, 46-foot tugboat, gift shop, and the spectacular Lens Exhibit Building, featuring the first-order lens from the Cape Canaveral Lighthouse. Contact:

> Ponce de Leon Inlet Lighthouse Museum
> 4931 South Peninsula Drive
> Ponce Inlet, FL 32127
> (904) 761-1821
> e-mail: lighthouse@ponceinlet.org
> website: http://www.ponceinlet.org

3) **Jupiter Inlet Lighthouse, Jupiter.** Designed and built by George Gordon Meade in 1860. First-order Fresnel lens, possibly the oldest in the state. Open Sunday through Wednesday 10:00 A.M. to 4:00 P.M. (last admission at 3:15 P.M.) Admission is $5.00. Includes small museum and gift shop. Contact:

> Jupiter Inlet Lighthouse
> c/o Florida History Center
> 805 U.S. Highway One
> Jupiter, FL 33477

(561) 747-8380

e-mail: grblanck@msn.com

website: http://www.members.aol.com/lightpic2/jupiter.html

4) **Cape Florida Lighthouse, Key Biscayne, at Bill Baggs Cape Florida State Recreation Area.** Built 1846; beautifully restored 1996. Open Thursday through Monday; tours at 10 A.M. and 1 P.M. Museum in keeper's dwelling and video in detached kitchen. Admission to park is $3.75 per car. Contact:

Bill Baggs Cape Florida State Recreation Area

1200 S. Crandon Boulevard

Key Biscayne, FL 33149

(305) 361-5811/361-8779

e-mail: capefla@gate.net

website: http://www.dep.state.fl.us/parks/district_5/billbaggs/index.html

5) **Key West Lighthouse, Key West.** Built 1847. Open daily 9:30 A.M. to 5:30 P.M. Admission is $6.00. Includes restored keeper's dwelling with museum, gift shop, and displays of several Fresnel lenses, including the first-order fixed lens from the Sombrero Reef Lighthouse. Contact:

Key West Lighthouse Museum

938 Whitehead Street

Key West, FL 33040

(305) 294-0012

e-mail: curatorcm@aol.com

website: http://www.kwahs.com/lighthouse.html

6) **Port Boca Grande (Gasparilla Island) Lighthouse, Gasparilla Island.** Built 1890. House-style lighthouse. Grounds open with access through Barrier Islands Geo Park. New lighthouse museum, gift shop, and lighthouse are open Wednesday through Sunday 10 A.M. to 4 P.M. Contact:

Boca Grande Lighthouse Museum

c/o Barrier Islands Geo Park

P.O. Box 1150

Boca Grande, FL 33921

(941) 964-0060

LIGHTHOUSES WITH GROUNDS OPEN ACCESSIBLE ONLY BY CAR

1) **Sanibel Island Lighthouse, Sanibel Island.** Lighthouse is on the grounds of city park. Lighthouse is closed, and keepers' dwellings are residences for city employees. Contact:

> City of Sanibel
> P.O. Drawer Q
> Sanibel, FL 33957

2) Boca Grande Rear Range Light, Gasparilla Island. Tower is fenced and closed. Located next to main road; easy access for photos along the beach. Contact:

> Boca Grande Lighthouse Museum
> c/o Barrier Islands Geo Park
> P.O. Box 1150
> Boca Grande, FL 33921
> (941) 964-0060

3) St. Marks Lighthouse. Access through St. Marks National Wildlife Refuge. Refuge is open 8 A.M. to 4:30 P.M., and there is an entrance fee. Contact:

> St. Marks National Wildlife Refuge
> P.O. Box 68
> St. Marks, FL 32355
> (904) 925-6121
> website: http://www.nettally.com/biernack/st.markslighthouse/st.marks/htm

4) Crooked River Lighthouse, Carabelle. Station has been abandoned, and access is by a dirt road off US 98, one mile west of Carabelle. Tower is not yet accessible, but public opening is anticipated. Contact:

> Barbara Revell
> Carrabelle Lighthouse Association
> P.O. Box 373
> Carrabelle, FL 32322
> (850) 697-2054
> e-mail: crkdrvrlh@aol.com
> website: http://www.geocities.com/carrabelle2000

5) Pensacola Lighthouse, Pensacola. Tower is open at times. Contact:

>   Dianne Levi
>   e-mail: dlg@gulfsurf.infi.net
>   website: http://cyberpensacola.com/cgaux/lighthouse.htm

LIGHTHOUSES WITH GROUNDS OPEN ACCESSIBLE ONLY BY BOAT

1) Dry Tortugas and Tortugas Harbor Lighthouses, Dry Tortugas. Also accessible by seaplane from Key West. Contact:

>   Fort Jefferson National Monument
>   P.O. Box 6208
>   Key West, FL 33040
>   (305) 242-7700
>   e-mail: ever_reception_desk@nps.gov
>   website: http://www.nps.gov/drto

2) Egmont Key Lighthouse, Egmont Key, near St. Petersburg. Contact:

>   Park Manager
>   Egmont Key State Park
>   4905 34th Street S. #5000
>   St. Petersburg, FL 33711
>   (813) 893-2627
>   e-mail: egmontkey@juno.com

3) Cape St. George Lighthouse, Apalachicola. Contact:

>   Cape St. George Lighthouse Society
>   P.O. Box 820
>   Apalachicola, FL 32329
>   (904) 653-8869
>   e-mail: stl@apalachtimes.com
>   website: http://apalachtimes.com/stl/index.html

LIGHTHOUSES NOT ACCESSIBLE
AT THIS TIME

1) Amelia Island Lighthouse, Fernandina, Florida. Currently under auspices of a Coast Guard Auxiliary, which does not permit visitors. Lighthouse can be seen, however, from Lighthouse Circle off Highland Street in Fernandina Beach. Contact:

> Amelia Island Lighthouse and Museum, Inc.
> 109 South 18th Street
> Fernandina, FL 32034
> (904) 261-3464
> e-mail: hal@net-magic.net

2) St. Johns River (Mayport) Lighthouse, Mayport, Florida. Lighthouse is in the process of being opened to the public. Visitors can get good views from the road near the Mayport ferry. Contact:

> Mayport Lighthouse Association, Inc.
> P.O. Box 35
> Mayport, FL 32267-0035
> (904) 251-2410
> fax (904) 251-3378
> e-mail: beaks@leading.net

3) Cape Canaveral Lighthouse, Cape Canaveral. Can be seen in passing from a NASA tour bus only. Contact:

> George H. Diller
> P.O. Box 21281
> Kennedy Space Center, FL 32815
> (407) 867-2468
> e-mail: george.diller_1@ksc.nasa.gov

4) Hillsboro Inlet Lighthouse, Hillsboro Beach and Pompano Beach. Can be seen from the Route A-1-A drawbridge over Hillsboro Inlet between Hillsboro Beach and Pompano Beach. Contact:

> Harry P. Cushing
> 2750 E. Atlantic Avenue

Pompano Beach, FL 33062
(954) 942-7263
e-mail: cushingiii@aol.com

5) Florida Reef Lights (Fowey Rocks, Carysfort Reef, Alligator Reef, Sombrero Key,
American Shoal, and Sand Key): May be approached by boat only. Contact:

Jerry Wilkinson
Historical Preservation Society of the Upper Keys
38 E. Beach Road
Tavernier, FL 33070
(305) 852-1620
e-mail: jerry142@terranova.net
website: http://www.keyshistory.org/caselighthouses.html

6) Anclote Keys Lighthouse, Anclote Key, near Tarpon Springs. The state is in the process of
taking over this lighthouse as part of a state park in the Anclote National Wildlife Refuge.
Lighthouse is currently off-limits while archeological and preservation processes are
ongoing. Contact:

Head Ranger
Gulf Islands GEO Park
#1 Causeway Drive
Dunedin, FL 34698
(727) 469-5942
website: http://www.dep.state.fl.us/parks/west/anclote.html

7) Cedar Keys Lighthouse, Seahorse Key, near Cedar Key. Lighthouse open only during
two-day open house in October. Contact:

Lower Suwannee and Cedar Keys National Wildlife Refuge
16450 N.W. 31 Place
Chiefland, FL 32626
(352) 493-0238
website: http://grove.ufl.edu/!aquajon/seahorse.htm

8) Cape San Blas Lighthouse, west of Apalachicola. Located on part of Eglin Air Force Base.
Cannot be seen from main road. Contact:

Director, Environmental Management
501 DeLeon Street
Building 696, Suite 101
Eglin Air Force Base, FL 32524-6802
(850) 882-4437

9) St. Joseph Point Lighthouse, south of Port St. Joe. Private residence.

CHRONOLOGICAL LIST OF ALL FLORIDA MANNED LIGHT STATIONS

(Roman numeral indicates lighthouse number if another tower existed on the same site before or after. Bold indicates towers still standing.)

Build date	Name	Status
1824	St. Augustine I	washed away in 1880
1824	Pensacola I:	torn down in 1860s
1825	Cape Florida I	torn down in 1846 to build new tower
1826	Key West I	blown down in hurricane in 1846
1826	Dry Tortugas I	(Garden Key): torn down in 1877
1827	Sand Key I	blown down in hurricane in 1846
1829	St. Marks I	not accepted by government; torn down to build St. Marks II
1830	St. Johns River I	torn down in 1833
1831	St. Marks II	torn down in 1842 to rebuild in new location
1833	St. Georges Island	torn down to build Cape St. George in 1847
1835	Mosquito Inlet I	washed away in 1836; not replaced until 1887
1835	St. Johns River II	replaced in 1859; fell down in 1920s
1839	Dog Island I	blown down in hurricane in 1842
1839	St. Joseph's Bay	torn down to build Cape San Blas in 1847
1839	**Amelia Island**	tower intact but new lantern installed after Civil War
1842	**St. Marks III**	tower extended and new lantern installed after Civil War
1843	Dog Island II	wooden tower blown down in hurricane in 1851
1846	**Cape Florida II**	tower extended with British-style lantern in 1855; discontinued in 1878 and replaced by Fowey Rocks

Build date	Name	Status
1847	Cape St. George I	washed away in hurricane in 1851
1847	**Key West II**	tower extended with new lantern in 1894; discontinued in 1969
1847	Cape San Blas I	washed away in hurricane in 1851
1847	Cape Canaveral I	replaced in 1868; torn down in 1894
1848	Egmont Key I	damaged in hurricanes; torn down in 1858
1852	**Cape St. George II**	tower intact with original lantern (oldest in Florida); discontinued in 1994
1852	Dog Island III	blown down in hurricane in 1873; replaced by Crooked River Lighthouse in 1895
1852	**Carysfort Reef**	tower intact with original lantern
1853	**Sand Key II**	tower intact with original lantern
1854	**Cedar Keys (Seahorse Key)**	tower intact with original lantern; discontinued in 1915
1854	Coffin's Patches	begun but destroyed in hurricane in 1856; replaced by Sombrero Key Lighthouse
1855	Northwest Passage I	torn down and rebuilt in 1878
1856	Cape San Blas II	blown down in hurricane in 1856
1858	**Egmont Key II**	tower intact but lantern removed after WWII
1858	**Sombrero Key**	tower intact with original lantern
1858	**Dry Tortugas II (Loggerhead Key)**	tower intact with original lantern
1859	**St. Johns River III**	tower intact but raised with new lantern in 1887; discontinued in 1929
1859	Cape San Blas III	fell into sea in 1882
1859	**Pensacola II**	tower intact with original lantern
1860	**Jupiter Inlet Lighthouse**	tower intact with original lantern
1868	**Cape Canaveral II**	tower intact with new dome on original lantern; tower moved in 1894
1872	Dames Point	discontinued in 1893; destroyed by fire in 1913

Build date	Name	Status
1873	**Alligator Reef**	tower intact with original lantern
1874	**St. Augustine II**	tower intact with original lantern
1876	**Tortugas Harbor**	tower intact with original lantern
1878	**Fowey Rocks**	tower intact with original lantern
1878	Northwest Passage II	discontinued in 1921; destroyed by fire in 1971 (pilings remain)
1880	**American Shoal**	tower intact with original lantern
1884	**Sanibel Island**	tower intact with original lantern
1885	**Cape San Blas IV**	tower intact with original lantern; moved in 1918; discontinued in 1996
1886	Volusia Bar	house burned in 1972 (pilings remain)
1886	Rebecca Shoal	house removed in 1953 (pilings remain)
1887	**Anclote Key**	tower intact with original lantern; discontinued in 1985
1887	**Mosquito (Ponce de Leon) Inlet II**	tower intact with original lantern
1890	**Port Boca Grande**	tower intact with original lantern
1890	Charlotte Harbor	discontinued and frame dwelling removed by 1935
1895	**Crooked River**	tower intact with original lantern; discontinued in 1996
1902	**St. Joseph Point**	discontinued in 1960s; house removed to location several miles south
1907	**Hillsboro Inlet**	tower intact with original lantern
1927	**Boca Grande Entrance Rear Range**	tower intact with original lantern
1954	**St. Johns River IV**	tower intact but original lantern removed in September 1998

FLORIDA'S FRESNEL LENSES

Bold indicates lighthouses remaining active with Fresnel lenses and the lenses that are known to be still in existence.

Amelia Island Lighthouse: 1868 Henry-LePaute third-order revolving Fresnel lens
  Characteristic: one white flash every 90 seconds
  Disposition: unknown
  ca. 1895 Barbier, Bénard third-order revolving Fresnel lens
  Installed in tower: October 24, 1903
  Characteristic: one white flash every 10 seconds, one red sector
  on the southeast
  Disposition: still active in tower

Amelia Island North Range Lighthouse: 1871 sixth-order fixed (red) Fresnel lens
  Manufacturer: unknown
  Characteristic: fixed red light
  Removed: 1899
  Disposition: unknown

St. Johns River (Mayport) Lighthouse: 1859 third-order fixed Fresnel lens
  Manufacturer: unknown but probably Henry-LePaute
  Characteristic: fixed white light with a red sector (red from 45° to 187°)
  Removed: 1929
  Disposition: unknown

Dames Point Lighthouse: 1872 fifth- or sixth-order fixed Fresnel lens
  Manufacturer: unknown
  Characteristic: fixed white light
  Removed: 1893
  Disposition: unknown

St. Augustine Lighthouse: 1871 L. Sautter et Lemonier first-order revolving panel lens
  Installed: 1874
  Characteristic: fixed light varied by flashes, one flash every 30 seconds
  Disposition: still active in tower
  Barbier, Bénard fourth-order fixed Fresnel lens similar to that
  used in old tower but of newer vintage

Date: ca. 1894–1901
Characteristic: fixed white light
Disposition: on display at St. Augustine Lighthouse Museum

Volusia Bar Lighthouse: 1886–1899 fourth-order fixed Fresnel lens
Manufacturer and date: unknown
Characteristic: fixed white light
Removed: 1899
Disposition: unknown
1899–1916 fifth-order fixed Fresnel lens
Manufacturer and date: unknown
Characteristic: fixed white light
Removed: 1916
Disposition: unknown

Ponce de Leon Inlet Lighthouse: **1867 Barbier et Fenestre fixed first-order lens**
Installed: 1887
Characteristic: fixed white light
Removed: 1933
Disposition: on display in Ponce de Leon Inlet Lighthouse Museum
1904 Barbier, Bénard et Turenne revolving third-order lens
Installed: 1933
Characteristic: group flashing, 6 flashes every 30 seconds
Removed: 1970
Disposition: on display in Ponce de Leon Inlet Lighthouse Museum

Cape Canaveral Lighthouse: **1860 Henry-LePaute first-order revolving lens**
Installed: 1868
Characteristic: white flash every 60 seconds (after 1936, one flash every 15 seconds)
Removed: for repair during lighthouse move of 1894 and returned to tower
Removed: 1993
Disposition: on display at Ponce de Leon Inlet Lighthouse Museum
Third-order lens set up on a fifty-foot structure during the moving of the lighthouse in 1894
Manufacturer and date: unknown
Disposition: unknown

Jupiter Inlet Lighthouse: 1858 L. Sautter et Co. first-order revolving lens

Installed: 1860 (After the Civil War, possibly returned to Montauk Lighthouse on Long Island, where it was originally intended to be installed)

Disposition: unknown

1863 Henry–LePaute first-order revolving lens

Installed: 1868

Characteristic: two one-second flashes every 30 seconds with 2 eclipses, one lasting 7.7 seconds, the other, 22.1 seconds

Disposition: still active in tower, possibly on L. Sautter pedestal

Hillsboro Inlet Lighthouse: 1906 Barbier, Bénard et Turenne Second-order revolving bivalve lens

Installed: 1907

Characteristic: flashing white every 20 seconds

Disposition: still active in tower

Cape Florida Lighthouse: 1855 Henry–LePaute second-order fixed Fresnel lens

Badly damaged in the Civil War and removed; afterwards the original second-order pedestal remained in lantern. It's possible that this lens may have been repaired and sent to the Grosse Point Lighthouse in Evanston, Illinois, but discrepancies make this seem highly unlikely.

Characteristic: fixed white light

Disposition: unknown

A new lens was installed after the Civil War, but its maker, type, date, and disposition are unknown. It was removed in 1878 when the lighthouse was abandoned in favor of the Fowey Rocks Lighthouse. As the Fowey Rocks Lighthouse used a first-order lens, it is unlikely that a second-order lens in Cape Florida could be transferred over to the new lighthouse.

1930s drum lens installed in 1978 when lighthouse was reactivated

Removed: 1988

Disposition: unknown

Fowey Rocks Lighthouse: **1876 Henry–LePaute first-order revolving Fresnel lens**

Characteristic: group flashing white (2), 3 red sectors

Removed: 1980s

Disposition: on display at the U.S. Coast Guard's Aid to Navigation School, Yorktown, Virginia

Carysfort Reef Lighthouse: **1857 Henry-LePaute first-order revolving lens**
    Installed: 1858
    Characteristic: group flashing white (3), 3 red sectors
    Removed: 1960s
    Disposition: on display at the Museum of Southern Florida History, Miami
    Henry-LePaute third-order fixed lens (date unknown)
    Installed: 1960s
    Removed: 1983
    Characteristic: (with flasher) group flashing white (3), 3 red sectors
    Disposition: on display at the Coast Guard Station, Miami Beach

Alligator Reef Lighthouse: 1873 first-order revolving Fresnel lens
    Manufacturer: unknown
    Characteristic: group flashing (4), 2 red sectors
    Disposition: destroyed in the 1935 Labor Day Hurricane (Several people in Islamorada have pieces of prisms.)

Sombrero Reef Lighthouse: **1857 Henry-LePaute first-order fixed Fresnel lens**
    Installed: 1858
    Characteristic: fixed white light; altered with flasher for group flashing (5), 3 red sectors
    Removed: 1980s
    Disposition: on display at the Key West Lighthouse Museum

American Shoal Lighthouse: 1874 Henry-LePaute first-order revolving Fresnel lens
    Characteristic: flashing white every 5 seconds, 3 red sectors
    Removed: 1980
    Disposition: unknown

Key West Lighthouse: 1858 Henry-LePaute third-order fixed Fresnel lens
    Installed: 1858
    Characteristic: fixed white light; altered with flasher to occulting white every 12 seconds, 3 red sectors
    Disposition: still in tower, active as a private aid to navigation

Sand Key Lighthouse: 1853 Henry-LePaute first-order revolving Fresnel lens
    Characteristic: group flashing white (2) every 10 seconds, 4 red sectors
    Removed: 1982
    Disposition: unknown

Northwest Passage Lighthouse: 1855 L. Sautter fifth-order fixed (white) Fresnel lens
    Characteristic: fixed white light
    Removed: 1921
    Disposition: unknown

Rebecca Shoal Lighthouse: 1886 fourth-order revolving (red and white) Fresnel lens
    Characteristic: one white and one red flash at 5-second intervals
    Damaged in storm and replaced
    Disposition: unknown
    1889 fourth-order revolving (red and white) Fresnel lens
    Characteristic: one white and one red flash at 5-second intervals
    Replaced: 1925
    Disposition: unknown
    1925 fourth-order revolving lens
    Characteristic: group flashing white (3) every 15 seconds, 1 red sector
    Removed: 1953
    Disposition: unknown

Tortugas Harbor Lighthouse: 1858 Henry-LePaute fourth-order fixed lens
    (Used first in the first Dry Tortugas Lighthouse, then moved into new 1876 iron tower)
    Removed: 1921
    Disposition: unknown

Dry Tortugas Lighthouse: 1858 L. Sautter and Co. first-order revolving Fresnel lens
    Characteristic: unknown
    Damaged in 1910 hurricane and replaced
    1910 Barbier, Bénard et Turenne second-order bivalve lens
    Installed: 1910
    Characteristic: flashing white every 20 seconds
    Removed: 1984; the mercury-float pedestal remains in tower
    Disposition: on display at the U.S. Coast Guard's Aid to Navigation School in Yorktown, Virginia

Sanibel Island Lighthouse: 1884 third-order revolving Fresnel lens
    Characteristic: unknown
    Removed: 1923; original pedestal remains in tower
    Disposition: unknown
    Third-order fixed Fresnel lens

Installed: 1923
Characteristic: (with flasher) group flashing white (2) every 10 seconds
Removed: 1962
Disposition: unknown
1920s Swedish-made fixed 500mm drum lens
Installed: 1923
Characteristic: group flashing white (2) every 10 seconds
Removed: 1990
Disposition: on display at the Sanibel Island Historical Village and Museum

Port Boca Grande Lighthouse: 1890 third-and-a-half-order revolving Fresnel lens
Characteristic: flashing white every 10 seconds
Removed: 1966
Disposition: unknown
375mm drum lens
Installed: 1988
Disposition: still in service

Boca Grande Entrance Rear Range Light: 1881 third-order fixed (red) Fresnel lens (Delaware)
Characteristic: fixed red light
Removed: 1918
Disposition: unknown (not used in Florida)
1932 fourth-order bivalve lens installed here in Florida
Characteristic: fixed red light
Removed: by 1943
Disposition: unknown

Charlotte Harbor Lighthouse: 1890 fifth-order fixed (red) Fresnel lens
Characteristic: fixed red light
Removed: by 1918
Disposition: unknown
Fifth-order revolving (white) Fresnel lens
Installed: by 1918
Characteristic: flashing white every second
Removed: ca. 1935
Disposition: unknown

Egmont Key Lighthouse: 1858 Henry-LePaute third-order fixed Fresnel lens
> *Characteristic:* fixed white light
> (Removed by Confederates during Civil War; unknown whether original lens or a similar one was re-installed)
> *Removed:* ca. 1944 (?)
> *Disposition:* unknown

Anclote Keys Lighthouse: 1887 Henry-LePaute third-order revolving Fresnel lens
> *Characteristic:* flashing white every 5 seconds
> *Removed:* 1960s
> *Disposition:* unknown

Cedar Keys Lighthouse: 1854 Henry-LePaute fourth-order fixed Fresnel lens
> (Lens removed by Confederates during Civil War; possibly replaced after the war)
> *Characteristic:* fixed white light
> *Removed:* 1915
> *Disposition:* unknown

St. Marks Lighthouse: 1867 Henry-LePaute fourth-order fixed lens
> *Characteristic:* fixed white light (altered with flasher to occulting white light every 4 seconds)
> *Disposition:* still active in tower

Dog Island: 1856 Henry-LePaute fourth-order revolving lens
> *Characteristic:* flashing white light
> (Removed during the Civil War and possibly replaced afterwards)
> *Disposition:* destroyed in hurricane of 1873

Crooked River: **1894 Henry-LePaute "⅓ open bivalve" lens**
> *Installed:* 1895
> *Characteristic:* group flashing white (2) every 12.5 seconds
> *Removed:* unknown
> *Disposition:* on display at the U.S. Coast Guard Eighth District Office in New Orleans

Cape St. George: 1857 Henry-LePaute third-order fixed lens
> *Characteristic:* fixed white light
> (Replaced in 1889 with a similar lens)

Disposition: unknown
Third-order lens installed in 1889
Manufacturer and date: unknown
Removed: unknown
Disposition: unknown

Cape San Blas Lighthouse: 1859 third-order revolving lens, possibly Henry-LePaute
(moved over from old tower)
> *Characteristic:* one white flash every 90 seconds
> *Removed:* 1906
> *Disposition:* unknown
> **1905 Barbier, Bénard et Turenne revolving third-order bivalve lens**
> *Installed:* 1906
> *Characteristic:* white flash every 20 seconds
> *Disposition:* remains in tower but no longer active. Original clockworks and weight also remain in tower, the only ones surviving in a Florida lighthouse!

St. Joseph Point Lighthouse: **1901 Barbier, Bénard et Turenne fixed third-order lens**
> *Characteristic:* fixed white light
> *Removed:* 1960
> *Disposition:* in storage at the Coast Guard facilities in Panama City Beach

Barrancas Rear Range Light: 1888 small fixed lens lantern (sixth-order?)
> *Removed:* 1930
> *Disposition:* unknown

Pensacola Lighthouse: 1858 Henry-LePaute first-order revolving lens
> *Characteristic:* flashing white light
> (Removed by Confederates in 1861)
> *Disposition:* recovered after the war but sent to New York for repair and never returned; final disposition unknown
> Fourth-order revolving lens installed in 1862 as temporary lens
> *Characteristic:* flashing white light
> *Removed:* 1869
> *Disposition:* unknown
> **1869 Henry-LePaute revolving first-order lens**
> *Installed:* 1869
> *Disposition:* still active in tower

Fort McRee Rear Range Light: 1888 small fixed lens lantern (sixth-order?)
   Characteristic: fixed white light
   Removed: 1930
   Disposition: unknown

ABOUT THE AUTHORS

Harold J. Belcher is a long-time resident of Fernandina Beach, Florida, a local historian, and president of the Amelia Island Lighthouse and Museum.

George Blanck is the executive director of the Florida History Center. He was instrumental in the restoration of the Jupiter Inlet Lighthouse.

Joan Gill Blank is a long-time resident of Key Biscayne, a noted historian, and author of *Key Biscayne: A History of Miami's Tropical Island and the Cape Florida Lighthouse.*

Hibbard Casselberry is one of Florida's most noted lighthouse enthusiasts and is a vice president of the Florida Lighthouse Association.

Love Dean (Winslow) is a resident of the Florida Keys, a noted historian, and author of several books about lighthouses, including *Lighthouses of the Florida Keys.*

Elinor De Wire is a nationally noted lighthouse historian and author of many lighthouse books, one of which, *Guide to Florida Lighthouses,* has become a standard.

Thomas M. Garner is the author of *The Pensacola Lighthouse* and recently served as the Northwest Florida District Commissioner for the Florida Lighthouse Association.

Marilyn Hoeckel serves with the Barrier Island Parks Society and has worked on the development of the museum at the Boca Grande (Gasparilla Island) Lighthouse.

Neil Hurley is a commander in the United States Coast Guard. He has published several books and many articles about lighthouses and is the creator of the website titled The Florida Lighthouse Page.

Richard Johnson is president of the Egmont Key Alliance and serves as secretary of the Florida Lighthouse Association.

Herman and Trip Jones are a father-and-son team who have been interested in the gulf coast lighthouses for many years and are major proponents of their preservation.

Janet and Scott Keeler have been instrumental in the preservation of the Anclote Keys Lighthouse. Scott is a reporter for the *St. Petersburg Times,* and his photographs of lighthouses have been displayed around the state.

Charles LeBuff lived for many years in the keeper's quarters of the Sanibel Island Lighthouse. He is a noted historian and author of local history.

John Lee is president of the Cape St. George Lighthouse Society and has been largely responsible for the effort to save the lighthouse, Florida's most endangered one.

Andrew M. Liliskis is president of the Mayport Lighthouse Association and the leading advocate for the opening of the St. Johns River (Mayport) Lighthouse to the public.

Danny Raffield and his family have been responsible for the preservation and restoration of the St. Joseph Point Lighthouse, which now serves as their residence.

Barbara Revell is president of the Carrabelle Lighthouse Association and the major proponent in the preservation of the Crooked River Lighthouse.

Thomas W. Taylor is historian at the Ponce de Leon Inlet Lighthouse and president of the Florida Lighthouse Association.

INDEX

ading this book, here are some other Pineapple Press titles you might enjoy
: our complete catalog or to place an order, write to Pineapple Press, P.O.
...asota, Florida 34230, or call 1-800-PINEAPL (746-3275). Or visit our website at www.pineapplepress.com.

Bansemer's Book of Florida Lighthouses by Roger Bansemer. This beautiful book depicts Florida's 30 lighthouses in over 200 paintings and sketches. Engaging text, historical tidbits, and charming sketches accompany full-color paintings. ISBN 1-56164-172-3 (hb)

Bansemer's Book of Carolina and Georgia Lighthouses by Roger Bansemer. Written and illustrated in the same engaging style as *Bansemer's Book of Florida Lighthouses,* this book accurately portrays how each lighthouse along the coasts of the Carolinas and Georgia looks today. ISBN 1-56164-194-4 (hb)

Guardians of the Lights by Elinor De Wire. Stories of the men and women of the U.S. Lighthouse Service. In a charming blend of history and human interest, this book paints a colorful portrait of the lives of a vanished breed. ISBN 1-56164-077-8 (hb); 1-56164-119-7 (pb)

Georgia's Lighthouses and Historic Coastal Sites by Kevin M. McCarthy. With full-color paintings by maritime artist William L. Trotter, this book retraces the history of 30 sites in the Peach State. ISBN 1-56164-143-X (pb)

Guide to Florida Lighthouses by Elinor De Wire. Its lighthouses are some of Florida's oldest and most historic structures, with diverse styles of architecture and daymark designs. ISBN 0-910923-74-4 (pb)

Key Biscayne: A History of Miami's Tropical Island and the Cape Florida Lighthouse by Joan Gill Blank. This is the engaging history of the southernmost barrier island in the United States and the Cape Florida Lighthouse, which has stood at Key Biscayne's southern tip for 170 years. ISBN 1-56164-103-0 (pb)

Lighthouses of the Carolinas by Terrance Zepke. Eighteen lighthouses aid mariners traveling the coasts of North and South Carolina. Here is the story of each, from origin to current status, along with visiting information and photographs. ISBN 1-56164-148-0 (pb)

Lighthouses of the Florida Keys by Love Dean. Intriguing, well-researched accounts of the shipwrecks, construction mishaps, natural disasters, and Indian attacks that plagued the Florida Keys' lighthouses and their keepers. ISBN 1-56164-160-X (hb); 1-56164-165-0 (pb)

Lighthouses of Ireland by Kevin M. McCarthy with paintings by William L. Trotter. Eighty navigational aids under the authority of the Commissioners of Irish Lights dot the 2,000 miles of Irish coastline. Each is addressed here, and 30 of the most interesting ones are featured with detailed histories and full-color paintings. ISBN 1-56164-131-6 (hb)